# A TESTAMENT
# OF DEVOTION

*by*
THOMAS R. KELLY

*With a Biographical Memoir by*
DOUGLAS V. STEERE

HARPER & ROW · PUBLISHERS
*New York and Evanston*

75 76 77 37 36 35 34 33 32

# TABLE OF CONTENTS

[ iii ]

## Acknowledgments

It is with the generous permission of the Friends Book Committee of 304 Arch Street, Philadelphia, that the lecture HOLY OBEDIENCE has been made available for inclusion here. The editors of THE FRIEND of the same address have given their consent for the reprinting of essays originally printed there. The friends of Thomas Kelly and especially E. Merrill Root, Rufus M. Jones, Mrs. A. L. Gillett, and John Cadbury have been most generous in supplying letters and material that furnished the substance for the biographical memoir. T. Canby Jones, T. Lloyd Cadbury and Albert L. Baily, Jr., have assisted with the reading of the proof. And finally, the publishers have taken more than a professional interest in the preparation of this little book for publication. I should like to express my thanks to each of those who have given such valuable assistance.

D. V. S.

## A Biographical Memoir

An adequate life, like Spinoza's definition of an adequate idea, might be described as a life which has grasped intuitively the whole nature of things, and has seen and felt and refocused itself to this whole. An inadequate life is one that lacks this adjustment to the whole nature of things—hence its twisted perspective, its partiality, its confusion. The story of Thomas Kelly's life is the story of a passionate and determined quest for adequacy. In the three years of his life that preceded his sudden death in January 1941, this search culminated in a rare degree of adequacy. The adequate life that he had known, he described with unusual simplicity and grace in the collection of his writings that are gathered in this slender volume.

Thomas Raymond Kelly was born on June 4, 1893 on a farm in southwestern Ohio near Chillicothe. His parents were ardent enough Quakers to have reopened an old Quaker meeting-house and to have revived a meeting for worship during their young married life. Thomas Kelly's father died when he was four, and in order to support him and his sister Mary, his mother worked the farm and delivered butter and eggs in the village for the next six years.

Then she moved to Wilmington, Ohio, in order that
the children might have the advantage of a good
school and later of a Quaker College. She learned
stenography and bookkeeping and started work in
the office of the Irwin Auger Bit Company at five
dollars a week to support her little family.

At Wilmington College Thomas Kelly was inci-
dentally absorbed in work to contribute to his own
support and in activities that helped to feed the religious hunger in his life, but centrally he was seized
there by a major loyalty. It was a loyalty to the physical sciences and especially to chemistry. If one was
to know the whole of life, here was a science that had
a precise method, that dared to accept what that
method turned up in spite of its rejection of previous
opinion, and whose magnificent achievements won by
the fearless use of such a method were evidence of
its greatness. As the laboratory assistant, he virtually
lived in the chemistry laboratory in his senior year
1912-13 at Wilmington College. He came on to
Haverford College for a year of further study, as
was often done by graduates of the Western Quaker
Colleges, and entered the senior class in 1913 con-
tinuing to do his major work in chemistry. At Haverford he came under the spell of Rufus Jones. In his
classroom he sensed the lure of philosophy and of
a search for truth in which his religious hunger and
his passion for science might both be given their due.

It was a glimpse ahead, but not yet realized for himself.

The avid hunger for life in this eager, intense, impetuous Quaker boy flared out on the first day of his arrival at Haverford from Ohio. Rufus Jones recalls his visit on that day, "When he was at Haverford as a student twenty-eight years ago, he came to my house deeply moved by his first day's stirring events. He sat down in front of me, his face lighted up with radiance and he said suddenly, 'I am just going to make my life a miracle!'"

The attachment to the sciences went on as he taught some science at Pickering College, a Quaker preparatory school in Canada during the two years from 1914-16 which he spent there. But hunger for life, the adequate life, made him open to the fascination of the kind of absolute commitment that was associated in the religious mind of that period with volunteering for service as a missionary. Canadian Friends had taken a particular interest in the Quaker Mission in Japan and Thomas Kelly decided to give himself to religious work in the Far East and entered Hartford Theological Seminary in the autumn of 1916 to prepare for it.

America's entry into the war stirred him to volunteer his services as a Quaker, first in canteen duty with the Y.M.C.A. and then in work with German prisoners of war in England where he spent from June

1917 to February 1918. The happy and moving experiences with the German prisoners drew him to a concern for the German people that was never to desert him. He took his Bachelor of Divinity degree at the Seminary in 1919. One of his colleagues there has forgotten any details of Thomas Kelly's years at the Seminary except that he was the gaiest, heartiest one of them all and that when there was any fun going, he could usually be found at the center of it.

At that period the Macy household, a Congregational clergyman's family, was an institution at the Hartford Theological Seminary. The father was himself a graduate of the Seminary, the son was a student there, and the daughters enjoyed high favor among the Seminary students. It was in his Seminary years that Thomas Kelly met Lael Macy. With an offer to return to his old college at Wilmington, Ohio, as a teacher of the Bible, he married her on the next day after his graduation in 1919. The war and the years of study had modified the mission goal, but the interest in Japan and the Far East continued. He spent two years at Wilmington College but he was restless to be on. In spite of the price that it would exact from him and from his loyal wife at that stage of his career, it was decided that he should prepare himself to teach philosophy and he was resolved that it must be a broad and a comprehensive enough philosophy to fathom Eastern as well as Western culture. He returned to Hartford Theological Seminary and spent three years with Professor A. L. Gillett giving himself to the study of philosophy. In June 1924 he secured his Ph.D. degree with a thesis on the place of value judgments in Lotze's philosophy

During these post-war years, the Quakers had been doing an extensive work in feeding German children and had established centers in a number of German cities. By 1924 the feeding work was being closed up and turned over to the local German social agencies, but it seemed wise to maintain the Quaker centers in Berlin and Vienna and to transform them into international centers where the Quaker spirit and way of life could be shared and from which Friends could perform any service that might open for them in the years ahead. The transition was a delicate one and required Quaker personnel of considerable spiritual maturity and wisdom. Thomas and Lael Kelly were chosen for this service in 1924 and spent fifteen months in Berlin giving themselves without reservation to the German Quakers and to the cultivation of this new type of center. Wilbur K. Thomas, the executive secretary of the American Friends Service Committee in those years, writes of this period of service in Germany, "The Center was in need of a strong, spiritual leader. Thomas R. Kelly was the man. His deep interest in spiritual problems, his sympathy with all who were troubled in spirit, his ability to interpret the religious message as emphasized by Friends, coupled with his executive ability, represented a contribution that cannot be emphasized too strongly."

In September 1925, Thomas and Lael Kelly returned from Germany to Richmond, Indiana, where Thomas Kelly had been called to teach philosophy at Earlham College. At the age of thirty-two he entered upon his teaching with a sense of his mission to place philosophy and the encouragement of rigorous reflective thinking in the high respect which it deserves in the education offered by a liberal arts college. His earlier passion for science had reappeared in his devotion to the philosophical method. There was to be no cutting of corners for any accepted views. Truth was to be discovered and acknowledged as such.

His most intimate friend at Earlham College, the poet, E. Merrill Root, writes of this period, "When I first knew him at Earlham, he was in rebellion against what seemed to him the churchliness or institutionalism of the self-consciously religious; he was a bit brash and brusque, I felt, and a bit too confident of the logical and scientific approach to truth . . . He always desired, and more ambitiously in his earlier years, to be a great scholar and to be associated with some college or university that lived by the austere and inexorable standards of excellence in truth which he set for himself. He wished, also and always, to be a living witness of truth; and whenever individuals, or meetings, or colleges, failed to incarnate his passionate desire for truth become flesh, he suffered. He was deeply sensitive and human and wrestled with his disappointments and despairs. He was not wholly happy in his last years at Earlham, because he desired a larger college or university where he could find students of more intense preparation and abilities."

There was a natural attractiveness and lovableness about Thomas Kelly that drew students and colleagues to him. His rich humor, all remember. "He laughed with the rich hearty abandon of wind and sun upon the open prairie. I have never heard richer, heartier laughter than his. He delighted in earth's incongruities, all the more perhaps because he saw eternal things and the values that transcend the earth . . . even the publicans and sinners among the students respected and loved him; he said to all, with Walt Whitman, 'Not till the sun refuses you do I refuse you.'"

A daughter, Lois, was born early in 1928 and the Kelly family built themselves a new home which they gaily shared with their student friends. But by 1930, the burning urge to be on with the quest, to broaden horizons, to extend opportunities led to a decision to study philosophy at what was still regarded as the most distinguished center in the United States, at

Harvard University. At great personal sacrifice and once again with the loyal encouragement of Lael Kelly, they gave up their new home, borrowed money and went to Cambridge, Massachusetts for the year. In 1931, he had an opportunity to fill a year's vacancy at Wellesley College while the professor of philosophy was on sabbatical leave. This meant opportunity for a further year of study at Harvard and he accepted it eagerly. He felt that his scholarship was getting the stimulus it had long lacked. At Wellesley in 1931-32 he not only taught the traditional courses and managed a seminar in Contemporary Realism, but supplemented the family income by preaching in a Congregational Church each Sunday at Fall River.

At Harvard the great event of the year was a course in directed reading under Professor A. N. Whitehead. It was in this reading that he conceived his first interest in the French philosopher, Emile Meyerson, upon whom he later wrote his only published book. He had taken a course in *Cosmologies Ancient and Modern* under Professor Whitehead the previous year and the turn of Professor Whitehead's thought grew on him and intrigued him. In June 1932, he wrote Professor A. L. Gillett, "I have begun to look in the direction of Whitehead for a richer analysis of the datum and find him tremendous." As Professor Whitehead talked, Thomas Kelly felt, as others have done, as though he were present at the day of creation and saw and shared in the whole drama, for there was no mistaking the fact that this great metaphysician possessed "a feeling of intimacy with the inside of the cosmos" to borrow a phrase of Justice Holmes. Professor Whitehead's child-fresh font of unusual and apt words that he minted to illuminate some experience also gripped Thomas Kelly and gave him new courage to allow himself great freedom in his own style of expression—a trait that is peculiarly striking in the devotional essays included in this volume.

Secretly there was the sharpest kind of hope that the two years at Harvard might bring with them an opening for teaching philosophy in some university in the East. But the spring of 1932 with its crushing economic depression wore on and the opportunity did not come. An offer to return to Earlham College had been generously held open until late spring, for Earlham College wanted Thomas Kelly to return. But to return seemed like renouncing the future and retreating into the past, and the decision to do it almost crushed Thomas Kelly. In June 1932, he wrote Professor Gillett of his letter of consent to return to Earlham College, "I cannot put into words what that letter cost me, but there is no use talking about it for there seems to be no other way." In August he was on top again and could write to the same friend that "the calibre of a man is found in his ability to meet disappointment successfully, enriched rather than narrowed by it." Once back at Earlham he gave himself to his teaching and to the spiritual and intellectual nurturing of a little group of students that used to gather at his home. John Cadbury and John Carter were two whose lives he influenced that year and they were not alone. He wrote to John Cadbury who had gone to Cornell University in 1933, "I wish we were nearer together in space and could have again an evening before the fire reading, discussing and meditating. The year has been going along in average mediocrity. There is no especial excellence, no especial defect in it. It's just it. And that's damnable. For the world is popping with novelty, adventure in ideas. And we aren't getting them here. We are safe and sane."

This last note represented the shadow of these second Earlham years. Many in this same period found in his teaching a source of great intellectual excitement. "He was a great teacher here, always eager, ardent, alive in the classroom. I remember still one of his students said in 1934, 'Professor Kelly is going to grow all the time.' That was the sense he gave his students."

But within him, there was the hunger for scholarly achievement and scholarly recognition that drove him on without relenting. The summer of 1932 he worked

on his book on Meyerson in the New York Public
Library and the Library at Columbia University. In
1933 he spent the entire summer in Widener Library
while his family lived in Maine. In 1934 he was invited by John Hughes to join the staff of the summer
school at Pendle Hill (a Quaker Center for Graduate
Religious and Social Study at Wallingford, Pennsylvania) and gave a course of lectures which he
called *The Quest for Reality*. "What a great month
it was," he wrote to a friend, "It was the first time I
felt 'released' . . . I only wish I could spend the
rest of the summer re-writing the stuff and seeing if
it could get into print."

But directly after the close of the summer school
he was at Widener Library again working on the
Meyerson manuscript. At Pendle Hill, the deeply
religious vein in him that his intimates at Earlham
knew and were greatly refreshed by, could pour
itself out unrestrained and use his scholarship as a
vehicle. But once out of this atmosphere, it was rigorous scholarship alone, he protested, that was the
goal of his heart's desire. In a letter to Professor
A. L. Gillett, he is almost savage in his intellectualist
declarations, "One thing is evident: I am hopelessly
committed to the life of a scholar. I'm not able to
be concerned primarily in practical problems of help-
fulness through organizations and classes but find the
current is irresistible in its flow toward the pole of

pure scholarship and research. . . . Lael tends to
think I am selfishly acquisitive in my attitude, but I
can't be anything but this kind of person, and I might
as well surrender to it." He wrote in the same tone to
Professor Clarence I. Lewis, his dearest personal
friend in the department of philosophy at Harvard,
"I merely want to write and work as a typical scholar
interested in the basic problems of research in meta-
physics and epistemology. . . . While the emphasis
I have laid is upon comprehensive world background
in philosophy, I rather expect writing will move in
the opposite direction, toward closer and more de-
tailed studies."

In the spring of 1935 he finished the manuscript
on Meyerson and at the same time made a decision
that promised to change the whole course of his life.
From the days of his missionary concern for Japan,
Thomas Kelly had had a steady interest for the culture of the Far East. At Earlham College, he had
sought to interest his student friends in the writings
and customs of the East. In the course of that spring
an opportunity came to go to the University of Hawaii
to teach philosophy and to assimilate what he could
of the atmosphere of China and Japan as it was reflected in this curious way-station between Orient and
Occident. After a long struggle to decide, he accepted
it. It seemed a step into the future again. He wrote
Professor Lewis of his reasons for the decision. "For

a number of years I have had a desire to be acquainted
with the philosophical thought of the whole world,
not merely with the thought of the Western world.
To live solely within one's own cultural traditions
(in this case, the outgrowths of Greek culture) not
actively familiar with the powerful thought of India,
China and the rest impresses me as a provincialism
not warranted by the spirit of philosophy itself. This
point of view was in my mind sometime before I
came to Harvard five years ago. And I laid out a tenta-
tive and hoped for course of life-development, which
had three steps or phases. The first phase was to get
an unimpeachable drill in the most rigorous philosophy department of the West. The second was to get
to the Orient, in some way or other, for a period of
two, three or four years (One can hardly compre-
hend the quest of the Buddha sitting under a maple
sugar tree in a mid-west corn field). The third was
to return to this country to teach and write with this
world-background."

Once established at the University of Hawaii in
the autumn of 1935, he saw Earlham becoming some-
what restored in stature. On first acquaintance, he
found the faculty there not as cultured or as culti-
vated as at Earlham. "If Earlham was over-benevolent
in its conceptions of a 'guarded' education, this institution is as far in the other direction." But closer
contact with several of his colleagues, with his more

able students, and especially with the Dean and the President whose vision for the institution he managed to catch, led him to temper his judgment before the year was out. The opportunity to associate with Chinese and Japanese scholars and the teaching of a course in Indian philosophy and a second in Chinese philosophy stirred up great enthusiasm in him. In a letter to Professor Rufus Jones, he says, "At a distance it might seem that the year here has been spent in a very restricted little field. I am reminded of the remark of a young fellow in Berlin who said to me, 'I never live an additional week in Berlin but what Bang! goes another horizon.' The horizons I have wanted to have broken, have been breaking and showing new and wonderful vistas."

A son, Richard Kelly had been born in Hawaii in February 1936. In March of that year Thomas Kelly was invited to join the philosophy department at Haverford College, to replace D. Elton Trueblood who had been called to be chaplain and Professor of the Philosophy of Religion at Stanford University. The offer was attractive. Thomas Kelly did not conceal his high opinion of Haverford College as he wrote Professor A. L. Gillett that "They go in for training young men of exceptionally promising ability and intellect . . . Their standards are high, blisteringly high."

In spite of its cutting short his plan of Eastern

studies, he accepted. For all of Hawaii's glorying in its climate, it had brought him nothing but miserable health. This was not new to him, for in the last years at Earlham he had paid the toll of his strenuous application. In the winter of 1933-34 he suffered severe attacks of kidney stones, and in January 1935 he was stricken with a siege of severe nervous exhaustion. During the whole late winter and spring of 1935, he got out of bed only to go to his classes and returned at once to rest again. Hawaii was to have restored him, but instead he developed an ugly sinus condition that necessitated an operation and he wrote to Professor A. L. Gillett about "being engaged in supporting the doctor. He has already well-nigh X-rayed me into the relief lines and heaven only knows what it will be in the long run."

The Kelly family arrived in Haverford early in September 1936. They swiftly found their place in the Quaker community. Thomas Kelly's gifts of ministry made themselves felt in Haverford Meeting. His sense of humor, however, did not desert him in coming among Eastern Quakers who called him from far and near to speak to their forums, commencements and classes. He wrote to a friend at this period, "An increasing number of speaking engagements come along, most of them highly unremunerative. Quakers with their unpaid ministry are well grounded in their Biblical persuasion that the Gospel is free." Nor was he uncritical of the annual gathering of Quakers that takes place in Philadelphia each spring, "Being a relative newcomer, I have no very good background for judging the Yearly Meeting at Arch Street. In the midst of a lot of historical lumber, I felt some life. But only a few have the vivid sense of the *freshness* and the *newness* of the Quaker discovery and emphasis. Was it not Gerald Heard who described Friends as reminding him of delicate chased silver. The explosive ruggedness of Luther and Fox is not found."

Thomas Kelly enjoyed his courses at Haverford College. This was especially true of his Greek philosophy and of a course in Oriental Philosophy which he inaugurated to carry on the interest that had taken him to Hawaii. At the time of his death he had interested one of the foundations in purchasing for the Haverford College Library extensive sets of reference books in Indian, Chinese and Japanese philosophy and culture. A course in the history and philosophy of Quakerism which he inherited from Rufus Jones gave him an occasion to immerse himself in Quaker history to his great delight. As a teacher at Haverford, he appealed to a small group of students whose enthusiasm for him and dedication to him knew few bounds. In the spring of 1938, he wrote to his faithful friend at Hartford, "I am more happy here at Haverford than anybody has a right to be, in this vale of tears and trouble(!) It is just about as ideal as one could ever wish for—yet with very human shortcomings."

In the first two years at Haverford, Little Richard Kelly was passing out of the baby stage. Lois Kelly, a beautiful girl of nine, was the idol of her father and reciprocated his affection. After the silent Quaker meeting for worship one day she told her mother that she had spent the meeting hour deciding whom she loved best, as she looked up at the gallery (where the elders of the meeting sit facing the meeting). After some weighing of the matter, she decided that she loved her daddy first, God second, Rufus Jones third, and J. Henry Bartlett fourth!

Thomas Kelly had done nothing with the manuscript on *Explanation and Reality in the Philosophy of Emile Meyerson* which because of its specialized character could never be published except under a heavy subsidy. This token of his intense period of scholarly application he felt determined to publish in spite of the expense involved which he could ill afford. It appeared in the late summer of 1937. It was well reviewed in the *Journal of Philosophy* and appreciated by the few competent to judge it. This book in some ways marked the culmination of seven tireless years of application to improve himself in scholarly attainment.

He had not been satisfied merely to receive the

stimulus of the department of philosophy at Harvard. He wanted also to have the stamp of their approval upon a work of his scholarship, perhaps ultimately to receive a Harvard degree. In the late autumn of 1937 after the publication of this book, a new life direction took place in Thomas Kelly. No one knows exactly what happened, but a strained period in his life was over. He moved toward adequacy. A fissure in him seemed to close, cliffs caved in and filled up a chasm, and what was divided grew together within him. Science, scholarship, method, remained good, but in a new setting. Now he could say with Isaac Pennington, "Reason is not sin but a deviating from that from which reason came is sin."

He went to the Germantown Friends' Meeting at Coulter Street to deliver three lectures in January 1938. He told me that the lectures wrote themselves. At Germantown, people were deeply moved and said, "This is *authentic*." His writings and spoken messages began to be marked by a note of experimental authority. "To you in this room who are seekers, to you, young and old who have toiled all night and caught nothing, but who want to launch out into the deeps and let down your nets for a draught, I want to speak as simply, as tenderly, as clearly as I can. For God *can* be found. There *is* a last rock for your souls, a resting place of absolute peace and joy and power and radiance and security.

There is a Divine Center into which your life can slip, a new and absolute orientation in God, a Center where you live with Him and out of which you see all of life, through new and radiant vision, tinged with new sorrows and pangs, new joys unspeakable and full of glory." It was the same voice, the same pen, the same rich imagery that always crowded his writing, and on the whole a remarkably similar set of religious ideas. But now he seemed to be expounding less as one possessed of *"knowledge about"* and more as one who had had unmistakable *"acquaintance with."* In April 1938, he wrote to Rufus Jones, "The reality of Presence has been very great at times recently. One knows at first hand what the old inquiry meant, 'Has Truth been advancing among you?'"

In 1935 Clarence Pickett and Rufus Jones on behalf of the American Friends Service Committee had tried to get Thomas Kelly to go back to Germany after ten years' absence and spend a summer visiting German Friends. His illness and his call to Hawaii made that impossible but now, in the summer of 1938, the call came again and he accepted. During this summer in Germany the ripening process went on apace as he lived in intimate fellowship with German Quakers and with others of all social classes. It was a religious journey, and like the earlier Friends, he went about from place to place and lived in Friends' homes talking out their problems with them, sitting in silence with them, and sharing his witness with them. He wrote a friend of the fellowship that summer where he knew and was known in that which is eternal, "I think, for example, of a day laborer in Stuttgart whom I visited recently. He knows the *Presence* so well. And we talked for a half an hour and stood together in silence and fully understood each other. He can't even speak correct German, but oh what a precious soul . . . I have had several long talks with the wife of a German, who has horny hands from desperately hard work. She loves the oppressed and the poor and the simple folk in a way that reminds me of St. Francis of Assisi. She knows the depths of the Divine Presence, the peace and creative power that you know, and through no grace of my own, I know also. Such consecration of life is amazing." He was later to write on this inward fellowship which was the social pole of his message in the last years of his life, "When we are drowned in the overwhelming seas of the love of God, we find ourselves in a new and particular relation to a few of our fellows."

He gave the Richard Cary Lecture at the German Yearly Meeting in 1938 presenting essentially the material which was included in his essay on *The Eternal Now and Social Concern.* It spoke to the condition of German Friends and they responded to him as they have scarcely done to any other American visitor. He left behind in Germany a memory that is still green.

To him, the German experience seemed to clarify still further what had come a few months before. He wrote to his mother at the close of that summer, "I am not at all as I was when I came to Germany, as you will find when you see me." In long visits that we had immediately upon his return in September 1938, he kept repeating, "It is wonderful. I have been literally melted down by the love of God." He told several of his student friends later of a specific experience that he had had on his knees in the great cathedral at Cologne where he seemed to feel God laying the whole congealed suffering of humanity upon his heart—a burden too terrible to be borne— but yet with His help bearable.

In a letter to Rufus Jones written on September 26th, 1938, he is eloquent on the experiences of the summer. "Two things have been very much on my mind about which I wanted to talk with thee . . . One thing was: I have had this summer, and still have, such a sweeping experience of 'refreshment of the spirit' so amazing, so sweet, and so prolonged as to go clear down to the roots of my being. The first verse of the Psalm I read in Meeting on First-day 'My soul was in a ferment and I was pricked in the reins of my heart' (Psalm 73:21) was intensely personal as thee probably recognized and I have longed to talk to thee about it. No, that is not quite the way to say it: rather I have longed to talk about *Him* who deals so tenderly and lovingly to undeserving hearts. For the inner fellowship, the Gebundenheit, the Verbundenheit of souls who know and who live by His Presence is very deep. It is the stuff out of which the Kingdom is made, is it not? . . . The first days here in America were days of *very* difficult readjustment, for I was very deeply immersed in the German world. But now I feel I must get reconnected."

The previous spring he had gone out to Albert Baily's farm with a group of seniors from Westtown School for a week-end retreat with them. They had had a moving time together and now one of these students, T. Canby Jones, was a freshman at Haverford College, and wished to continue the fellowship. He and several of his friends began coming over to Thomas Kelly's home one evening each week to talk and read together of books of mutual interest. They lived on a mixed diet of St. Augustine's *Confessions* and Gibran's *The Prophet* for the first few weeks and had an easy time of silence together after the readings. During the next two years they read a number of books of devotional literature together. Pere Grou, Meister Eckhart, Brother Lawrence, Letters by a Modern Mystic, The Little Flowers of St.

Francis, and then, quite naturally, the New Testament and the Psalms. The group grew until it often had six or seven students. At times no one would appear. But Thomas Kelly was always on hand. He found in this close spiritual fellowship that developed, one of the greatest comforts of his life. One of the students describes the group, "Tom, of course, was always telling funny stories even about the deepest thoughts. We met when we felt the need, not definitely once a week, but usually so. Tom often spoke of dry periods, but he as often described with a radiant face the degrees of ecstasy one achieves when he is wholly committed to God. In the Spring of 1939, Tom expressed his concern for message-bearing. He told us many times he wanted us to be a band of itinerant preachers and expressed the desire that groups like ours be started everywhere: spiritual dynamos for the revitalization of meetings and the church. The idea grew that this gathering of such cells, more than speaking should be our task . . . In short, our group was a little religious order. Grounded in seeking God and the meaning of life, rejoicing in the love for each other, and thankful for the life that resulted from that corporate search." It is a tribute to the vitality of this group that they have continued to meet after Thomas Kelly's death and have added several other seekers to their number.

As the experience of this inward life matured,

Thomas Kelly found himself using language that would have repelled him during his years of rebellion against evangelical religion. "Have I discovered God as a sweet Presence and a stirring life-renovating Power within me? Do I walk by His Guidance feeding every day, like the knights of the Grail on the body and the blood of Christ?" An Earlham colleague wrote of his visit there in the autumn of 1940, "He almost startled me, and he shocked some of us who were still walking in the ways of logic and science and the flesh, by the high areas of being he had penetrated. He had returned to old symbols like the blood of Christ, that were shocking to a few of his old colleagues who had not grown and lived as he had. But he brought new meaning to all symbols, and he was to me, and to some others a prophet whose tongue had been touched by coals of fire."

As his experience ripened, there also came a growing reemphasis upon the centrality of *devotion*, a devotion that far exceeds the mere possession of inward states of exaltation: "Let us be quite clear that mystical exaltations are not essential to religious dedication . . . Many a man professes to be without a shred of mystical elevation, yet is fundamentally a heaven-dedicated soul. It would be a tragic mistake to suppose that religion is only for a small group, who have certain vivid but transient inner experiences, and to preach those experiences so that those

who are relatively insensitive to them should feel
excluded, denied access to the Eternal love, deprived
of a basic necessity for religious living. The crux of
religious living lies in the *will*, not in transient and
variable states. Utter dedication of will to God is
open to *all* . . . Where the will to will God's will
is present, there is a child of God. When there
are graciously given to us such glimpses of glory as
aid us in softening own-will, then we may be humbly
grateful. But glad willing away of self that the will
of God, so far as it can be discerned, may become
what we will—that is the basic condition.[1]

There was no withdrawal from life during these
years. Thomas Kelly found in the American Friends
Service Committee a corporate means of expression
with which he felt deep unity. His concern was central in the establishment of the Quaker Center at
Shanghai and he guided a little committee that met
often to scrutinize the Eastern scene. He also became
chairman of the Fellowship Council and as such
served for two years on the Board of Directors of
the Service Committee.

The literary harvest of this period was not long in
coming. Most of it was printed in *The Friend*, a
Quaker religious and literary journal published bi-
weekly in Philadelphia. *The Eternal Now and Social
Concern* appeared in March 1938; the Richard Cary

[1] *The Gathered Meeting,* The Friend, December 12, 1940, p. 205.

Lecture, *Das Ewige in seiner Gegenwart und Zeitliche Führung,* containing similar material, was published in German in August 1938, the counsel on *Simplicity* appeared in a symposium on that subject in March 1939; the *Blessed Community* in September 1939. Three striking essays on Quakerism, not included in this volume, appeared in the same journal between 1938 and 1940: *Quakers and Symbolism, The Quaker Discovery,* and *The Gathered Meeting.* In late March 1939, Thomas Kelly delivered the annual William Penn Lecture, entitled *Holy Obedience,* to the Yearly Meeting of Quakers. This lecture was read in religious circles throughout the United States and brought requests for more devotional material of this authentic character.

Nine days before his death, he wrote me a letter which he sent to Portugal by clipper. In it he described the last piece of writing he was to do. "Spent last week (vacation) writing in bare hope of publication, on practical procedure and conduct of the self in living by, and oriented toward, the Light within, both in private devotion and in public reaction to the world of men and events, seeing them in and through the Light . . . Read one at Pendle Hill last Sunday." These three chapters of rare grace and suggestiveness form the opening chapters of this little collection.

He died very suddenly of a heart attack on January 17, 1941 at the age of forty-seven years. His friend, E. Merrill Root, wrote to Lael Kelly from Earlham College, "I cannot tell you adequately, and yet I think you know, how much I loved Tom. He was my great friend and comrade here; there was no one else who entered the inner circle of the heart, or shared the heights of the soul. He was the perfect friend, whether we shared the gay sunlight of humor, or ascended the peaks of highest vision together. I had especially marvelled to see how he grew always in insight and power, and rejoiced at the light he brought me and all men. He was a great strength to me. The thought of him was always a beatitude, a great light, a wind of courage."

A neighbor in Maine who had watched with admiration Thomas Kelly's skill with carpenters' tools, and who looked forward to his evening visits, wrote simply, "I will find it very difficult to realize that he will not wander over with his lantern next summer and tarry with us for a while to bless and cheer us."

Gerald Heard, who had never met Thomas Kelly but who had been moved by his devotional writing, wrote to a mutual friend at the news of Thomas Kelly's death, "I was filled with a kind of joy when I read of Thomas Kelly. It was formerly the custom of the Winston Salem Community of Moravians in North Carolina to announce the passing of a member by the playing of three chorales by the church band from the top of the church tower. So I feel I want to sing when I hear of such men emerging. I know it is an outward loss to us—though even directly we may gain more than we lose by their joining the more active side of the communion of saints—but I keep on feeling what it must be for a man as good as he to be able to push aside this fussy veil of the body and look unblinking at the Light, never again, maybe, to be distracted, unintentional, unaware, always concentrated."

These devotional essays are gathered here without any of the cutting or clipping or the critical revision which Thomas Kelly would certainly have given them had he lived. They are all written on the same theme and often develop an identical aspect, but always with some fresh illumination. Few can resist feeling the power of the current that is in this stream. They are in very truth a testament of devotion.

Haverford, Pennsylvania
April 10, 1941.

DOUGLAS V. STEERE

## The Light Within

Meister Eckhart wrote, "As thou art in church or cell, that same frame of mind carry out into the world, into its turmoil and its fitfulness." Deep within us all there is an amazing inner sanctuary of the soul, a holy place, a Divine Center, a speaking Voice, to which we may continuously return. Eternity is at our hearts, pressing upon our time-torn lives, warming us with intimations of an astounding destiny, calling us home unto Itself. Yielding to these persuasions, gladly committing ourselves in body and soul, utterly and completely, to the Light Within, is the beginning of true life. It is a dynamic center, a creative Life that presses to birth within us. It is a Light Within which illumines the face of God and casts new shadows and new glories upon the face of men. It is a seed stirring to life if we do not choke it. It is the Shekinah of the soul, the Presence in the midst. Here is the Slumbering Christ, stirring to be awakened, to become the soul we clothe in earthly form and action. And He is within us all.

You who read these words already know this inner Life and Light. For by this very Light within you, is your recognition given. In this humanistic age we suppose man is the initiator and God is the responder.

But the Living Christ within us is the initiator and we are the responders. God the Lover, the accuser, the revealer of light and darkness presses within us. "Behold I stand at the door and knock." And all our apparent initiative is already a response, a testimonial to His secret presence and working within us.

The basic response of the soul to the Light is internal adoration and joy, thanksgiving and worship, self-surrender and listening. The secret places of the heart cease to be our noisy workshop. They become a holy sanctuary of adoration and of self-oblation, where we are kept in perfect peace, if our minds be stayed on Him who has found us in the inward springs of our life. And in brief intervals of overpowering visitation we are able to carry the sanctuary frame of mind out into the world, into its turmoil and its fitfulness, and in a hyperaesthesia of the soul, we see all mankind tinged with deeper shadows, and touched with Galilean glories. Powerfully are the springs of our will moved to an abandon of singing love toward God; powerfully are we moved to a new and overcoming love toward time-blinded men and all creation. In this Center of Creation all things are ours, and we are Christ's and Christ is God's. We are owned men, ready to run and not be weary and to walk and not faint.

But the light fades, the will weakens, the humdrum returns. Can we stay this fading? No, nor should we try, for we must learn the disciplines of His will, and pass beyond this first lesson of His Grace. But the Eternal Inward Light does not die when ecstasy dies, nor exist only intermittently, with the flickering of our psychic states. Continuously renewed immediacy, not receding memory of the Divine Touch, lies at the base of religious living. Let us explore together the secret of a deeper devotion, a more subterranean sanctuary of the soul, where the Light Within never fades, but burns, a perpetual Flame, where the wells of living water of divine revelation rise up continuously, day by day and hour by hour, steady and transfiguring. The "bright shoots of everlastingness" can become a steady light within, if we are deadly in earnest in our dedication to the Light, and are willing to pass out of first stages into maturer religious living. Only if this is possible can the light from the inner sanctuary of the soul be a workaday light for the marketplace, a guide for perplexed feet, a recreator of culture-patterns for the race of men.

What is here urged are internal practices and habits of the mind. What is here urged are secret habits of unceasing orientation of the deeps of our being about the Inward Light, ways of conducting our inward life so that we are perpetually bowed in worship, while we are also very busy in the world of daily affairs. What is here urged are inward practices of the mind at deepest levels, letting it swing like the needle, to the polestar of the soul. And like the needle, the Inward Light becomes the truest guide of life, showing us new and unsuspected defects in ourselves and our fellows, showing us new and unsuspected possibilities in the power and life of goodwill among men. But, more deeply, He who is within us urges, by secret persuasion, to such an amazing Inward Life with Him, so that, firmly cleaving to Him, we always look out upon all the world through the sheen of the Inward Light, and react toward men spontaneously and joyously from this Inward Center. Yield yourself to Him who is a far better teacher than these outward words, and you will have found the Instructor Himself, of whom these words are a faint and broken echo.

Such practice of inward orientation, of inward worship and listening, is no mere counsel for special religious groups, for small religious orders, for special "interior souls," for monks retired in cloisters. This practice is the heart of religion. It is the secret, I am persuaded, of the inner life of the Master of Galilee. He expected this secret to be freshly discovered in everyone who would be his follower. It creates an amazing fellowship, the church catholic and invisible, and institutes group living at a new level, a society grounded in reverence, history rooted in eternity, colonies of heaven.

It is the special property of no group or sect, but is a universal obligation and privilege. Roman Catholics have treasured this practice, but have overlaid the authority of the Light Within by a heavy weight of external ecclesiastical authority. Protestant emphasis, beginning so nobly in the early Luther, has grown externally rationalistic, humanistic, and service-minded. Dogmas and creed and the closed revelation of a completed canon have replaced the emphasis upon keeping close to the fresh upspringings of the Inner Life. The dearth of rich Protestant literature on the interior aspect of Christian living, except as it bears on the opening experience of conversion, bears testimony to its emphasis being elsewhere.

The Society of Friends arose as a rediscovery of the ever-open inward springs of immediacy and revelation. George Fox and the Quakers found a Principle within men, a Shekinah of the soul, a Light Within that lights every man coming into the world. Dedicating themselves utterly and completely to attendance upon this Inward Living Christ, they were quickened into a new and bold tenderness toward the blindness of the leaders of Christian living. Aflame with the Light of the inner sanctuary, they went out into the world, into its turmoil and its fitfulness, and called men to listen above all to that of God speaking within them, to order all life by the Light of the Sanctuary. "Dear Friends," writes Fox to his groups, "keep close to that which is pure within you, which leads you up to God." John Woolman, the Quaker tailor of Mt. Holly, New Jersey, resolved so to order his outward affairs, so to adjust his business burdens, that nothing, absolutely nothing would crowd out his prime attendance upon the Inward Principle. And in this sensitizing before the inward altar of his soul, he was quickened to see and attack effectively the evils of slave-holding, of money-loaning, of wars upon the Indians.

But the value of Woolman and Fox and the Quakers of today for the world does not lie merely in their outward deeds of service to suffering men, it lies in that call to all men to the practice of orienting their entire being in inward adoration about the springs of immediacy and ever fresh divine power within the secret silences of the soul. The Inner Light, the Inward Christ, is no mere doctrine, belonging peculiarly to a small religious fellowship, to be accepted or rejected as a mere belief. It is the living Center of Reference for all Christian souls and Christian groups—yes, and of non-Christian groups as well ·—who seriously mean to dwell in the secret place of the Most High. He is the center and source of action, not the end-point of thought. He is the locus of commitment, not a problem for debate. Practice comes first in religion, not theory or dogma. And Christian practice is not exhausted in outward deeds. These are the fruits, not the roots. A practicing Christian must above all be one who practices the perpetual return of the soul into the inner sanctuary, who brings the world into its Light and rejudges it, who brings the Light into the world with all its turmoil and its fitfulness and recreates it (after the pattern seen on the Mount). To the reverent exploration of this practice we now address ourselves.

II

There is a way of ordering our mental life on more than one level at once. On one level we may be thinking, discussing, seeing, calculating, meeting all the demands of external affairs. But deep within, behind the scenes, at a profounder level, we may also be in prayer and adoration, song and worship and a gentle receptiveness to divine breathings.

The secular world of today values and cultivates only the first level, assured that *there* is where the real business of mankind is done, and scorns, or smiles in tolerant amusement, at the cultivation of the second level—a luxury enterprise, a vestige of superstition, an occupation for special temperaments. But in a deeply religious culture men know that the deep level of prayer and of divine attendance is the

most important thing in the world. It is at this deep
level that the real business of life is determined. The
secular mind is an abbreviated, fragmentary mind,
building only upon a part of man's nature and neglect-
ing a part—the most glorious part—of man's nature,
powers and resources. The religious mind involves
the whole of man, embraces his relations with time
within their true ground and setting in the Eternal
Lover. It ever keeps close to the fountains of divine
creativity. In lowliness it knows joys and stabilities,
peace and assurances, that are utterly incomprehen-
sible to the secular mind. It lives in resources and
powers that make individuals radiant and triumphant,
groups tolerant and bonded together in mutual concern, and is bestirred to an outward life of unremit-
ting labor.

Between the two levels is fruitful interplay, but
ever the accent must be upon the deeper level, where
the soul ever dwells in the presence of the Holy One.
For the religious man is forever bringing all affairs
of the first level down into the Light, holding them
there in the Presence, reseeing them and the whole
of the world of men and things in a new and over-
turning way, and responding to them in spontaneous,
incisive and simple ways of love and faith. Facts
remain facts, when brought into the Presence in the
deeper level, but their value, their significance, is
wholly realigned. Much apparent wheat becomes

utter chaff, and some chaff becomes wheat. Imposing powers? They are out of the Life, and must crumble. Lost causes? If God be for them, who can be against them? Rationally plausible futures? They are weakened or certified in the dynamic Life and Light. Tragic suffering? Already He is there, and we actively move, in His tenderness, toward the sufferers. Hopeless debauchees? These are children of God, His concern and ours. Inexorable laws of nature? The dependable framework for divine reconstruction. The fall of a sparrow? The Father's love. For faith and hope and love for all things are engendered in the soul, as we practice their submission and our own to the Light Within, as we humbly see all things, even darkly and as through a glass, yet through the eye of God.

But the upper level of our mind plays upon the deeper level of divine immediacy of internal communion and of prayer. It furnishes us with the objects of divine concern, "the sensualized material of our duty," as Fichte called it. It furnishes us with those culture-patterns of our group which are at one and the same time the medium and the material for their regeneration, our language, our symbols, our traditions, and our history. It provides for the mystic the suggestions for his metaphors, even the metaphor of the Light, the Seed, the Sanctuary, whereby he would suggest and communicate the wonder of God's immediacy and power. It supplies the present-day tools of reflection whereby the experience of Eternity is knit into the fabric of time and thought. But theologies and symbols and creeds, though inevitable, are transient and become obsolescent, while the Life of God sweeps on through the souls of men in continued revelation and creative newness. To that divine Life we must cling. In that Current we must bathe. In that abiding yet energizing Center we are all made one, behind and despite the surface differences of our forms and cultures. For the heart of the religious life is in commitment and worship, not in reflection and theory.

How, then, shall we lay hold of that Life and Power, and live the life of prayer without ceasing? By quiet, persistent practice in turning of all our being, day and night, in prayer and inward worship and surrender, toward Him who calls in the deeps of our souls. Mental habits of inward orientation must be established. An inner, secret turning to God can be made fairly steady, after weeks and months and years of practice and lapses and failures and returns. It is as simple an art as Brother Lawrence found it, but it may be long before we achieve any steadiness in the process. Begin now, as you read these words, as you sit in your chair, to offer your whole selves, utterly and in joyful abandon, in quiet, glad surrender to Him who is within. In secret ejaculations of praise, turn in humble wonder to the Light, faint though it may be. Keep contact with the outer world of sense and meanings. Here is no discipline in absent-mindedness. Walk and talk and work and laugh with your friends. But behind the scenes, keep up the life of simple prayer and inward worship. Keep it up throughout the day. Let inward prayer be your last act before you fall asleep and the first act when you awake. And in time you will find as did Brother Lawrence, that "those who have the gale of the Holy Spirit go forward even in sleep."

The first days and weeks and months are awkward and painful, but enormously rewarding. Awkward, because it takes constant vigilance and effort and reassertions of the will, at the first level. Painful, because our lapses are so frequent, the intervals when we forget Him so long. Rewarding, because we have begun to live. But these weeks and months and perhaps even years must be passed through before He gives us greater and easier stayedness upon Himself.

Lapses and forgettings are so frequent. Our surroundings grow so exciting. Our occupations are so exacting. But when you catch yourself again, lose no time in self-recriminations, but breathe a silent prayer for forgiveness and begin again, just where you are. Offer *this* broken worship up to Him and say: "This is what I am except Thou aid me." Admit no discouragement, but ever return quietly to Him and wait in His Presence.

At first the practice of inward prayer is a process of alternation of attention between outer things and the Inner Light. Preoccupation with either brings the loss of the other. Yet what is sought is not alternation, but simultaneity, worship undergirding every moment, living prayer, the continuous current and background of all moments of life. Long practice indeed is needed before alternation yields to concurrent immersion in both levels at once. The "plateaus in the learning curve" are so long, and many falter and give up, assenting to alternation as the best that they can do. And no doubt in His graciousness God gives us His gifts, even in intermittent communion, and touches us into flame, far beyond our achievements and deserts. But the hunger of the committed one is for unbroken communion and adoration, and we may be sure He longs for us to find it and supplements our weakness. For our quest is of His initiation, and is carried forward in His tender power and completed by His grace.

The first signs of simultaneity are given when at the moment of recovery from a period of forgetting there is a certain sense that we have not completely forgotten Him. It is as though we are only coming back into a state of vividness which had endured in dim and tenuous form throughout. What takes place now is not reinstatement of a broken prayer but return to liveliness of that which had endured, but mildly. The currents of His love have been flowing, but whereas we had been drifting in Him, now we swim. It is like the background of a picture which extends all the way across behind a tree in the foreground. It is not that we merely know intellectually that the background of the picture has unbroken extension; we experience aesthetically that it *does* extend across. Again, it is like waking from sleep yet knowing, not by inference but by immediate awareness, that we have lived even while we were asleep. For sole preoccupation with the world is sleep, but immersion in Him is life.

But periods of dawning simultaneity and steadfast prayer may come and go, lapsing into alternation for long periods and returning in glorious power. And we learn to submit to the inner discipline of withdrawing of His gifts. For if the least taint of spiritual pride in our prayer-growth has come, it is well that He humble us until we are worthy of greater trust. For though we begin the practice of secret prayer with a strong sense that we are the initiators and that by our wills we are establishing our habits, maturing experience brings awareness of being met, and tutored, purged and disciplined, simplified and made pliant in His holy will by a power waiting within us. For God Himself works in our souls, in their deepest depths, taking increasing control as we are progressively willing to be prepared for His wonder. We cease trying to make ourselves the dictators and God the listener, and become the joyful listeners to Him, the Master who does all things well.

There is then no need for fret when faithfully turning to Him, if He leads us but slowly into His secret chambers. If He gives us increasing steadiness in the deeper sense of His Presence, we can only quietly thank Him. If He holds us in the stage of alternation we can thank Him for His loving wisdom, and wait upon His guidance through the stages for which we are prepared. For we cannot take Him by storm. The strong man must become the little child, not understanding but trusting the Father.

But to some at least He gives an amazing stayedness in Him, a well-nigh unbroken life of humble quiet adoration in His Presence, in the depths of our being. Day and night, winter and summer, sunshine and shadow, He is here, the great Champion. And we are with Him, held in His Tenderness, quickened into quietness and peace, children in Paradise before the Fall, walking with Him in the garden in the heat as well as the cool of the day. Here is not ecstasy but serenity, unshakableness, firmness of life-orientation. We are become what Fox calls "established men."

Such men are not found merely among the canonized Saints of the Church. They are the John Woolmans of today. They are housewives and hand workers, plumbers and teachers, learned and unlettered,

black and white, poor and perchance even rich. They
exist, and happy is the church that contains them.
They may not be known widely, nor serve on boards
of trustees, or preach in pulpits. Where pride in one's
learning is found, there they are not. For they do
not confuse acquaintance with theology and church
history with commitment and the life lived in the
secret sanctuary. Cleaving simply through forms and
externals, they dwell in immediacy with Him who is
the abiding Light behind all changing forms, really
nullifying much of the external trappings of religion.
They have found the secret of the Nazarene, and,
not content to assent to it intellectually, they have
committed themselves to it in action, and walk in
newness of life in the vast fellowship of unceasing
prayer.

There is no new technique for entrance upon this
stage where the soul in its deeper levels is continuously at Home in Him. The processes of inward
prayer do not grow more complex, but more simple.
In the early weeks we begin with simple, whispered
words. Formulate them spontaneously, "Thine only.
Thine only." Or seize upon a fragment of the Psalms:
"so panteth my soul after Thee, O God." Repeat them
inwardly, over and over again. For the conscious co-
operation of the surface level is needed at first,
before prayer sinks into the second level as habitual
divine orientation. Change the phrases, as you feel

led, from hour to hour or from forenoon to afternoon.
If you wander, return and begin again. But the time
will come when verbalization is not so imperative,
and yields place to the attitudes of soul which you
meant the words to express, attitudes of humble bow-
ing before Him, attitudes of lifting high your whole
being before Him that the Light may shine into the
last crevice and drive away all darkness, attitudes
of approach and nestling in the covert of His wings,
attitudes of amazement and marvel at His transcend-
ent glory, attitudes of self-abandonment, attitudes of
feeding in an inward Holy Supper upon the Bread
of Life. If you find, after a time, that these attitudes
become diffused and vague, no longer firm-textured,
then return to verbalizations and thus restore their
solidity.

But longer discipline in this inward prayer will establish more enduring upreachings of praise and submission and relaxed listening in the depths, unworded
but habitual orientation of all one's self about Him
who is the Focus. The process is much simpler now.
Little glances, quiet breathings of submission and
invitation suffice. Voluntary or stated times of prayer
merely join into and enhance the steady undercurrent
of quiet worship that underlies the hours. Behind the
foreground of the words continues the background of
heavenly orientation, as all the currents of our being

set toward Him. Through the shimmering light of divine Presence we look out upon the world, and in its turmoil and its fitfulness, we may be given to respond, in some increased measure, in ways dimly suggestive of the Son of Man.

We may suppose these depths of prayer are our achievement, the precipitate of our own habits at the surface level settled into subconscious regions. But this humanistic account misses the autonomy of the life of prayer. It misses the fact that this inner level has a life of its own, invigorated not by us but by a divine Source. There come times when prayer pours forth in volumes and originality such as we cannot create. It rolls through us like a mighty tide. Our prayers are mingled with a vaster Word, a Word that at one time was made flesh. We pray, and yet it is not we who pray, but a Greater who prays in us. Something of our punctiform selfhood is weakened, but never lost. All we can say is, Prayer is taking place, and I am given to be in the orbit. In holy hush we bow in Eternity, and know the Divine Concern tenderly enwrapping us and all things within His persuading love. Here all human initiative has passed into acquiescence, and He works and prays and seeks His own through us, in exquisite, energizing life. Here the autonomy of the inner life becomes complete and we are joyfully *prayed through*, by a Seeking Life that flows through us into the world of men. Sometimes this prayer is particularized, and we are impelled to pray for particular persons or particular situations with a quiet or turbulent energy that, subjectively considered, seems utterly irresistible. Sometimes the prayer and this Life that flows through us reaches out to all souls with kindred vision and upholds them in His tender care. Sometimes it flows out to the world of blinded struggle, and we become cosmic Saviors, seeking all those who are lost.

This "infused prayer" is not frequently given, in full intensity. But something of its autonomous character remains, not merely as a memory of a time when the fountains of creation were once revealed and we were swept along in their rising waters. It remains as an increasing awareness of a more-than-ourselves, working persuadingly and powerfully at the roots of our own soul, and in the depths of all men. It is an experimental assurance of Divine Labor and persuasion pervading the world, impelling men to their cross. In holy awe we are drawn anew to "keep close to the fresh up-springings of the Life," amazed at that which is revealed as at work, at the base of all being, all men and ourselves. And we have our firsthand assurance that He who began that good work in us, as in Timothy, can establish us in Him, can transform intermittency and alternation into simultaneity and continuity.

III

Guidance of life by the Light within is not exhausted as is too frequently supposed, in special leadings toward particular tasks. It begins first of all in a mass revision of our total reaction to the world. Worshipping in the light we become new creatures, making wholly new and astonishing responses to the entire outer setting of life. These responses are not reasoned out. They are, in large measure, spontaneous reactions of felt incompatibility between "the world's" judgments of value and the Supreme Value we adore deep in the Center. There is a total Instruction as well as specific instructions from the Light within. The dynamic illumination from the deeper level is shed upon the judgments of the surface level, and lo, the "former things are passed away, behold, they are become new."

Paradoxically, this total Instruction proceeds in two opposing directions at once. We are torn loose from earthly attachments and ambitions—*contemptus mundi*. And we are quickened to a divine but painful concern for the world—*amor mundi*. He plucks the world out of our hearts, loosening the chains of attachment. And He hurls the world into our hearts, where we and He together carry it in infinitely tender love.

The second half of the paradox is more readily accepted today than the first. For we fear it means world-withdrawal, world-flight. We fear a life of wallowing in ecstasies of spiritual sensuality while cries of a needy world go unheeded. And some pages of history seem to fortify our fears.

But there is a sound and valid *contemptus mundi* which the Inner Light works within the utterly dedicated soul. Positions of prominence, eminences of social recognition which we once meant to attain— how puny and trifling they become! Our old ambitions and heroic dreams—what years we have wasted in feeding our own insatiable self-pride, when only His will truly matters! Our wealth and property, security now and in old age—upon what broken reeds have we leaned, when He is "the rock of our heart, and our portion forever!"

Again, we have quailed and been tormented in our obscurity, we have fretted and been anxious because of our limitations, set by our own nature and by our surroundings. The tasks are so great, and we have accomplished so little, and been assigned such lowly talents and occupations.

But instructed in one point of view of the paradox, we bestride the mountains or the valleys of earthly importance with a holy indifference, contempt, and detachment. Placed in coveted surroundings, recipients of honors, we count them as refuse, as nothing, utterly nothing. Placed in the shadows, we are happy to pick up a straw for the love of God. No task is so small as to distress us, no honor so great as to turn our heads.

Such loosening of the chains of attachment is easy, if we be given times of a sense of unutterable nearness to Himself. In those moments what would we not leave for Him? What mean honors or dishonors, comforts or wants, in Him? For some persons, in such moments, the work of detachment, *contemptus mundi,* exists chiefly as an intellectual obligation, ominously hovering over their heads as duty, but not known as experienced joy in the new freedom of utter poverty. Still others obstruct this detachment, reject it as absurd or unneeded, and cling to mammon while they seek to cling to God.

Double-mindedness in this matter is wholly destructive of the spiritual life. Totalitarian are the claims of Christ. No vestige of reservation of "our" rights can remain. Straddle arrangements and compromises between our allegiances to the surface level and the divine Center cannot endure. Unless the willingness is present to be stripped of our last earthly dignity and hope, and yet still praise Him, we have no message in this our day of refugees, bodily and spiritual. Nor have we yielded to the monitions of the Inner Instructor.

But actually completed detachment is vastly harder

than intended detachment. Fugitive islands of secret
reservations elude us. Rationalizations hide them. In-
tending absolute honesty, we can only bring ourselves
steadfastly into His presence and pray, "Cleanse thou
me from secret faults." And in the X-ray light of
Eternity we may be given to see the dark spots of life,
and divine grace may be given to reinforce our will
to complete abandonment in Him. For the guidance
of the Light is critical, acid, sharper than a two-edged
sword. He asks all, but He gives all.

## Holy Obedience

Out in front of us is the drama of men and of nations, seething, struggling, laboring, dying. Upon this tragic drama in these days our eyes are all set in anxious watchfulness and in prayer. But within the silences of the souls of men an eternal drama is ever being enacted, in these days as well as in others. And on the outcome of this inner drama rests, ultimately, the outer pageant of history. It is the drama of the Hound of Heaven baying relentlessly upon the track of man. It is the drama of the lost sheep wandering in the wilderness, restless and lonely, feebly searching, while over the hills comes the wiser Shepherd. For His is a shepherd's heart, and He is restless until He holds His sheep in His arms. It is the drama of the Eternal Father drawing the prodigal home unto Himself, where there is bread enough and to spare. It is the drama of the Double Search, as Rufus Jones calls it. And always its chief actor is—the Eternal God of Love.

It is to one strand in this inner drama, one scene, where the Shepherd has found His sheep, that I would direct you. It is the life of absolute and complete and holy obedience to the voice of the Shepherd. But ever throughout the account the accent will be laid upon

God, God the initiator, God the aggressor, God the seeker, God the stirrer into life, God the ground of our obedience, God the giver of the power to become children of God.

## I. THE NATURE OF HOLY OBEDIENCE

Meister Eckhart wrote: "There are plenty to follow our Lord half-way, but not the other half. They will give up possessions, friends and honors, but it touches them too closely to disown themselves." It is just this astonishing life which is willing to follow Him the other half, sincerely to disown itself, this life which intends *complete* obedience, without *any* reservations, that I would propose to you in all humility, in all boldness, in all seriousness. I mean this literally, utterly, completely, and I mean it for you and for me—commit your lives in unreserved obedience to Him.

If you don't realize the revolutionary explosiveness of this proposal you don't understand what I mean. Only now and then comes a man or a woman who, like John Woolman or Francis of Assisi, is willing to be utterly obedient, to go the other half, to follow God's faintest whisper. But when such a commitment comes in a human life, God breaks through, miracles are wrought, world-renewing divine forces are released, history changes. There is nothing more important now than to have the human race endowed with just such committed lives. Now is no time to say, "Lo, here. Lo, there." Now is the time to say, "Thou art the man." To this extraordinary life I call you— or He calls you through me—not as a lovely ideal, a charming pattern to aim at hopefully, but as a serious, concrete program of life, to be lived here and now, in industrial America, by you and by me.

This is something wholly different from mild, conventional religion which, with respectable skirts held back by dainty fingers, anxiously tries to fish the world out of the mudhole of its own selfishness. Our churches, our meeting houses are full of such respectable and amiable people. We have plenty of Quakers to follow God the first half of the way. Many of us have become as mildly and as conventionally religious as were the church folk of three centuries ago, against whose mildness and mediocrity and passionlessness George Fox and his followers flung themselves with all the passion of a glorious and a new discovery and with all the energy of dedicated lives. In some, says William James, religion exists as a dull habit, in others as an acute fever. Religion as a dull habit is not that for which Christ lived and died.

There is a degree of holy and complete obedience and of joyful self-renunciation and of sensitive listening that is breath-taking. Difference of degree passes over into utter difference of kind, when one tries to follow Him the second half. Jesus put this pointedly when He said, "Ye must be born again" (John 3:3), and Paul knew it: "If any man is in Christ, he is a new creature" (2 Cor. 5:17).

George Fox as a youth was religious enough to meet all earthly standards and was even proposed as a student for the ministry. But the insatiable God-hunger in him drove him from such mediocrity into a passionate quest for the real whole-wheat Bread of Life. Sensible relatives told him to settle down and get married. Thinking him crazy, they took him to a doctor to have his blood let—the equivalent of being taken to a psychiatrist in these days, as are modern conscientious objectors to war in Belgium and France. Parents, if some of your children are seized with this imperative God-hunger, don't tell them to snap out of it and get a job, but carry them patiently in your love, or at least keep hands off and let the holy work of God proceed in their souls. Young people, you who have in you the stirrings of perfection, the sweet, sweet rapture of God Himself within you, be faithful to Him until the last lingering bit of self is surrendered and you are wholly God-possessed.

The life that intends to be wholly obedient, wholly submissive, wholly listening, is astonishing in its completeness. Its joys are ravishing, its peace profound, its humility the deepest, its power world-shaking, its love enveloping, its simplicity that of a trusting child.

It is the life and power in which the prophets and apostles lived. It is the life and power of Jesus of Nazareth, who knew that "when thine eye is single thy whole body is full of light" (Luke 11:34). It is the life and power of the apostle Paul, who resolved not to know anything among men save Jesus Christ and Him crucified. It is the life and power of Saint Francis, that little poor man of God who came nearer to re-living the life of Jesus than has any other man on earth. It is the life and power of George Fox and of Isaac and Mary Penington. It is the life and power and utter obedience of John Woolman who decided, he says, "to place my whole trust in God," to "act on an inner Principle of Virtue, and pursue worldly business no farther than as Truth opened my way therein." It is the life and power of myriads of unknown saints through the ages. It is the life and power of some people now in this room who smile knowingly as I speak. And it is a life and power that can break forth in this tottering Western culture and return the Church to its rightful life as a fellowship of creative, heaven-led souls.

## II. Gateways into Holy Obedience

In considering one gateway into this life of holy obedience, let us dare to venture together into the inner sanctuary of the soul, where God meets man in awful immediacy. There is an indelicacy in too-ready speech. Paul felt it unlawful to speak of the things of the third heaven. But there is also a false reticence, as if these things were one's own work and one's own possession, about which we should modestly keep quiet, whereas they are wholly God's amazing work and we are nothing, mere passive receivers. "The lion hath roared, who can but tremble? The voice of Jehovah hath spoken, who can but prophesy?" (Amos 3:8).

Some men come into holy obedience through the gateway of profound mystical experience.

It is an overwhelming experience to fall into the hands of the living God, to be invaded to the depths of one's being by His presence, to be, without warning, wholly uprooted from all earth-born securities and assurances, and to be blown by a tempest of unbelievable power which leaves one's old proud self utterly, utterly defenseless, until one cries, "All Thy waves and thy billows are gone over me" (Ps. 42:7). Then is the soul swept into a Loving Center of ineffable sweetness, where calm and unspeakable peace and ravishing joy steal over one. And one knows now why Pascal wrote, in the center of his greatest moment, the single word, "Fire." There stands the world of struggling, sinful, earth-blinded men and nations, of plants and animals and wheeling stars of heaven, all new, all lapped in the tender, persuading

Love at the Center. There stand the saints of the ages, their hearts open to view, and lo, their hearts are our heart and their hearts are the heart of the Eternal One. In awful solemnity the Holy One is over all and in all, exquisitely loving, infinitely patient, tenderly smiling. Marks of glory are upon all things, and the marks are cruciform and blood-stained. And one sighs, like the convinced Thomas of old, "My Lord and my God" (John 20:28). Dare one lift one's eyes and look? Nay, whither *can* one look and not see Him? For field and stream and teeming streets are full of Him. Yet as Moses knew, no man can look on God and live—live as his old self. Death comes, blessed death, death of one's alienating will. And one knows what Paul meant when he wrote, "The life which I now live in the flesh I live by the faith of the Son of God" (Gal. 2:20).

One emerges from such soul-shaking, Love-invaded times into more normal states of consciousness. But one knows ever after that the Eternal Lover of the world, the Hound of Heaven, is utterly, utterly real, and that life must henceforth be forever determined by that Real. Like Saint Augustine one asks not for greater certainty of God but only for more steadfastness in Him. There, beyond, in Him is the true Center, and we are reduced, as it were, to nothing, for He is all.

Is religion subjective? Nay, its soul is in objectivity,

in an Other whose Life is our true life, whose Love is our love, whose Joy is our joy, whose Peace is our peace, whose burdens are our burdens, whose Will is our will. Self is emptied into God, and God in-fills it. In glad, amazed humility we cast on Him our little lives in trusting obedience, in erect, serene, and smiling joy. And we say, with a writer of Psalms, "Lo, I come: in the book of the law it is written of me, I delight to do Thy will, O my God" (Ps. 40:7-8). For nothing else in all of heaven or earth counts so much as His will, His slightest wish, His faintest breathing. And holy obedience sets in, sensitive as a shadow, obedient as a shadow, selfless as a shadow. Not reluctantly but with ardor one longs to follow Him the second half. Gladly, urgently, promptly one leaps to do His bidding, ready to run and not be weary and to walk and not faint.

Do not mistake me. Our interest just now is in the life of complete obedience to God, not in amazing revelations of His glory graciously granted only to some. Yet the amazing experiences of the mystics leave a permanent residue, a God-subdued, a God-possessed will. States of consciousness are fluctuating. The vision fades. But holy and listening and alert obedience remains, as the core and kernel of a God-intoxicated life, as the abiding pattern of sober, workaday living. And some are led into the state of complete obedience by this well-nigh passive route, wherein God alone seems to be the actor and we seem to be wholly acted upon. And our wills are melted and dissolved and made pliant, being firmly fixed in Him, and He wills in us.

But in contrast to this passive route to complete obedience most people must follow what Jean-Nicholas Grou calls the active way, wherein *we* must struggle and, like Jacob of old, wrestle with the angel until the morning dawns, the active way wherein the will must be subjected bit by bit, piecemeal and progressively, to the divine Will.

But the first step to the obedience of the second half is the flaming vision of the wonder of such a life, a vision which comes occasionally to us all, through biographies of the saints, through the journals of Fox and early Friends, through a life lived before our eyes, through a haunting verse of the Psalms—"Whom have I in heaven but Thee? And there is none upon earth that I desire beside Thee" (Ps. 73:25)—through meditation upon the amazing life and death of Jesus, through a flash of illumination or, in Fox's language, a great opening. But whatever the earthly history of this moment of charm, this vision of an absolutely holy life is, I am convinced, the invading, urging, inviting, persuading work of the Eternal One. It is curious that modern psychology cannot account wholly for flashes of insight of any kind, sacred or secular. It is as if a fountain of creative Mind were welling up, bubbling to expression within prepared spirits. There is an infinite fountain of lifting power, pressing within us, luring us by dazzling visions, and we can only say, The creative God comes into our souls. An increment of infinity is about us. Holy is imagination, the gateway of Reality into our hearts. The Hound of Heaven is on our track, the God of Love is wooing us to His Holy Life.

Once having the vision, the second step to holy obedience is this: Begin where you are. Obey *now*. Use what little obedience you are capable of, even if it be like a grain of mustard seed. Begin where you are. Live this present moment, this present hour as you now sit in your seats, in utter, utter submission and openness toward Him. Listen outwardly to these words, but within, behind the scenes, in the deeper levels of your lives where you are all alone with God the Loving Eternal One, keep up a silent prayer, "Open thou my life. Guide my thoughts where I dare not let them go. But Thou darest. Thy will be done." Walk on the streets and chat with your friends. But every moment behind the scenes be in prayer, offering yourselves in continuous obedience. I find this internal continuous prayer life absolutely essential. It can be carried on day and night, in the thick of business, in home and school. Such prayer of submission can be so simple. It is well to use a single sentence, repeated over and over and over again, such as this: "Be Thou my will. Be Thou my will," or "I open all before Thee. I open all before Thee," or "See earth through heaven. See earth through heaven." This hidden prayer life can pass, in time, beyond words and phrases into mere ejaculations, "My God, my God, my Holy One, my Love," or into the adoration of the Upanishad, "O Wonderful, O Wonderful, O Wonderful." Words may cease and one stands and walks and sits and lies in wordless attitudes of adoration and submission and rejoicing and exultation and glory.

And the third step in holy obedience, or a counsel, is this: If you slip and stumble and forget God for an hour, and assert your old proud self, and rely upon your own clever wisdom, don't spend too much time in anguished regrets and self-accusations but begin again, just where you are.

Yet a fourth consideration in holy obedience is this: Don't grit your teeth and clench your fists and say, "I will! I will!" Relax. Take hands off. Submit yourself to God. Learn to live in the passive voice— a hard saying for Americans—and let life be willed through you. For "I will" spells not obedience.

## III. HUMILITY AND HOLINESS

The fruits of holy obedience are many. But two are so closely linked together that they can scarcely be treated separately. They are the passion for per-

sonal holiness and the sense of utter humility. God
inflames the soul with a craving for absolute purity.
But He, in His glorious otherness, empties us of ourselves in order that He may become all.

Humility does not rest, in final count, upon baffle-
ment and discouragement and self-disgust at our
shabby lives, a brow-beaten, dog-slinking attitude. It
rests upon the disclosure of the consummate wonder
of God, upon finding that only God counts, that all
our own self-originated intentions are works of straw.
And so in lowly humility we must stick close to the
Root and count our own powers as nothing except as
they are enslaved in His power.

But O how slick and weasel-like is self-pride! Our
learnedness creeps into our sermons with a clever
quotation which adds nothing to God's glory, but a
bit to our own. Our cleverness in business competi-
tion earns as much self-flattery as does the possession
of the money itself. Our desire to be known and ap-
proved by others, to have heads nod approvingly
about us behind our backs, and flattering murmurs
which we can occasionally overhear, confirm the discernment in Alfred Adler's elevation of the superi-
ority motive. Our status as "weighty Friends" gives us
secret pleasures which we scarcely own to ourselves,
yet thrive upon. Yes, even pride in our own humility
is one of the devil's own tricks.

But humility rests upon a holy blindedness, like

the blindedness of him who looks steadily into the sun. For wherever he turns his eyes on earth, there he sees only the sun. The God-blinded soul sees naught of self, naught of personal degradation or of personal eminence, but only the Holy Will working impersonally through him, through others, as one objective Life and Power. But what trinkets we have sought after in life, the pursuit of what petty trifles has wasted our years as we have ministered to the enhancement of our own little selves! And what needless anguishes we have suffered because *our* little selves were defeated, were not flattered, were not cozened and petted! But the blinding God blots out this self and gives humility and true selfhood as wholly full of Him. For as He gives obedience so He graciously gives to us what measure of humility we will accept. Even that is not our own, but His who also gives us obedience. But the humility of the God-blinded soul endures only so long as we look steadily at the Sun. Growth in humility is a measure of our growth in the habit of the Godward-directed mind. And he only is near to God who is exceedingly humble. The last depths of holy and voluntary poverty are not in financial poverty, important as that is; they are in poverty of spirit, in meekness and lowliness of soul.

Explore the depths of humility, not with your intellects but with your lives, lived in prayer of humble obedience. And there you will find that humility is not merely a human virtue. For there is a humility that is in God Himself. Be ye humble as God is humble. For love and humility walk hand in hand, in God as well as in man.

But there is something about deepest humility which makes men bold. For utter obedience is self-forgetful obedience. No longer do we hesitate and shuffle and apologize because, say we, we are weak, lowly creatures and the world is a pack of snarling wolves among whom we are sent as sheep by the Shepherd (Matt. 10:16). I must confess that, on human judgment, the world tasks we face are appalling—well-nigh hopeless. Only the inner vision of God, only the God-blindedness of unreservedly dedicated souls, only the utterly humble ones can bow and break the raging pride of a power-mad world. But self-renunciation means God-possession, the being possessed by God. Out of utter humility and self-forgetfulness comes the thunder of the prophets, "Thus saith the Lord." High station and low are leveled before Him. Be not fooled by the world's power. Imposing institutions of war and imperialism and greed are wholly vulnerable for they, and we, are forever in the hands of a conquering God. These are not cheap and hasty words. The high and noble adventures of faith can in our truest moments be seen as no adventures at all, but certainties. And if we live in complete humility in God we can smile in patient assurance as we work. Will you be wise enough and humble enough to be little fools of God? For who can finally stay His power? Who can resist His persuading love? Truly says Saint Augustine, "There is something in humility which raiseth the heart upward." And John Woolman says, "Now I find that in the pure obedience the mind learns contentment, in appearing weak and foolish to the wisdom which is of the World; and in these lowly labors, they who stand in a low place, rightly exercised under the Cross, will find nourishment."

But God inflames the soul with a burning craving for absolute purity. One burns for complete innocency and holiness of personal life. No man can look on God and live, live in his own faults, live in the shadow of the least self-deceit, live in harm toward His least creatures, whether man or bird or beast or creeping thing. The blinding purity of God in Christ, how captivating, how alluring, how compelling it is! The pure in heart shall see God? More, they who see God shall cry out to become pure in heart, even as He is pure, with all the energy of their souls.

This has been an astonishing and unexpected element for me. In this day of concern for social righteousness it sounds like a throwback to medieval ideals of saintliness and soul-combing. Our religious heroes of these social gospel days sit before a battery

of telephones, with full office equipment, with tele-
graph lines to Washington and London and Tokyo
and Berlin. And this is needed, desperately needed.
Yet there is in the experience of God this insistent,
imperative, glorious yearning—the craving for complete spotlessness of the inner self before Him.

No average goodness will do, no measuring of
our lives by our fellows, but only a relentless, inexorable divine standard. No relatives suffice; only abso-
lutes satisfy the soul committed to holy obedience.
Absolute honesty, absolute gentleness, absolute self-
control, unwearied patience and thoughtfulness in the
midst of the raveling friction of home and office and
school and shop. It is said that the ermine can be
trapped by surrounding it with a circle of filth. It
will die before it will sully its snowy coat. Have we
been led astray by our fears, by the fear of saccharine
sweetness and light? By the dangers of fanatical
scrupulousness and self-inspection and halo-hunting?
By the ideal of a back-slapping recommendation of
religion by showing we were good fellows after all?
By the fear of quietism and of that monastic retreat
from the world of men's needs which we associate
with medieval passion for holiness of life? Nay,
tread not so far from the chasm that you fall into
the ditch on the other side. Boldly must we risk the
dangers which lie along the margins of excess, if we
would live the life of the second half. For the life of

obedience is a holy life, a separated life, a renounced life, cut off from worldly compromises, distinct, heaven-dedicated in the midst of men, stainless as the snows upon the mountain tops.

He who walks in obedience, following God the second half, living the life of inner prayer of submission and exultation, on him God's holiness takes hold as a mastering passion of life. Yet ever he cries out in abysmal sincerity, "I am the blackest of all the sinners of the earth. I am a man of unclean lips, for mine eyes have seen the King, Jehovah of Hosts." For humility and holiness are twins in the astonishing birth of obedience in the heart of men. So God draws unworthy us, in loving tenderness, up into fellowship with His glorious self.

## IV. ENTRANCE INTO SUFFERING

Another fruit of holy obedience is entrance into suffering. I would not magnify joy and rapture, although they are unspeakably great in the committed life. For joy and rapture need no advocates. But we shrink from suffering and can easily call all suffering an evil thing. Yet we live in an epoch of tragic sorrows, when man is adding to the crueler forces of nature such blasphemous horrors as drag soul as well as body into hell. And holy obedience must walk in this world, not aloof and preoccupied, but stained with sorrow's travail.

Nor is the God-blinded soul given blissful oblivion but, rather, excruciatingly sensitive eyesight toward the world of men. The sources of suffering for the tendered soul are infinitely multiplied, well-nigh beyond all endurance. Ponder this paradox in religious experience: "Nothing matters; everything matters." I recently had an unforgettable hour with a Hindu monk. He knew the secret of this paradox which we discussed together: "Nothing matters; everything matters." It is a key of entrance into suffering. He who knows only one-half of the paradox can never enter that door of mystery and survive.

There is a lusty, adolescent way of thought among us which oversimplifies the question of suffering. It merely says, "Let us remove it." And some suffering can, through more suffering, be removed. But there is an inexorable residue which confronts you and me and the blighted souls of Europe and China and the Near East and India, awful, unremovable in a lifetime, withering all souls not genuinely rooted in Eternity itself. The Germans call it *Schicksal* or Destiny. Under this word they gather all the vast forces of nature and disease and the convulsive upheavals of social life which sweep them along, as individuals, like debris in a raging flood, into an unknown end. Those who are not prepared by the inner certitude of

Job, "I know that my Avenger liveth" (Job 19:25), must perish in the flood.

One returns from Europe with the sound of weeping in one's ears, in order to say, "Don't be deceived. *You* must face Destiny. Preparation is only possible now. Don't be fooled by your sunny skies. When the rains descend and the floods come and the winds blow and beat upon *your* house, your private dwelling, your own family, your own fair hopes, your own strong muscles, your own body, your own soul itself, then it is well-nigh too late to build a house. You can only go inside what house you have and pray that it is founded upon the Rock. Be not deceived by distance in time or space, or the false security of a bank account and an automobile and good health and willing hands to work. Thousands, perhaps millions as good as you have had all these things and are perishing in body and, worse still, in soul today."

An awful solemnity is upon the earth, for the *last vestige* of earthly security is gone. *It has always been gone,* and religion has always said so, but we haven't believed it. And some of us Quakers are not yet undeceived, and childishly expect our little cushions for our little bodies, in a world inflamed with untold ulcers. Be not fooled by the pleasantness of the Main Line life, and the niceness of Germantown existence, and the quiet coolness of your well-furnished homes. For the plagues of Egypt are upon the world, entering hovel and palace, and there is no escape for you or for me. There is an inexorable amount of suffering in all life, blind, aching, unremovable, not new but only terribly intensified in these days.

One comes back from Europe aghast at having seen how lives as graciously cultured as ours, but rooted only in time and property and reputation, and self-deluded by a mild veneer of religious respectability but unprepared by the amazing life of commitment to the Eternal in holy obedience, are now doomed to hopeless, hopeless despair. For if you will accept as normal life only what you can understand, then you will try only to expel the dull, dead weight of Destiny, of inevitable suffering which is a part of normal life, and never come to terms with it or fit your soul to the collar and bear the burden of *your* suffering which must be borne by you, or enter into the divine education and drastic discipline of sorrow, or rise radiant in the sacrament of pain.

One comes back from Europe to plead with you, you here in these seats, you my pleasant but often easy-living friends, to open your lives to such a baptism of Eternity now as turns this world of tumbling change into a wilderness in your eyes and fortifies you with an unshakable peace that passes all understanding and endures all earthly shocks without soul-destroying rebelliousness. Then and then only can we, weaned from earth, and committed wholly to God alone, hope to become voices crying in this wilderness of Philadelphia and London, "Prepare ye the way of the Lord. Make straight in this desert a highway for our God" (Isa. 40:3). These are old truths. But now is no time for enticing novelties but for a return to the everlasting truths of life and suffering and Eternity and unreserved commitment to Him who is over all.

The heart is stretched through suffering, and enlarged. But O the agony of this enlarging of the heart, that one may be prepared to enter into the anguish of others! Yet the way of holy obedience leads out from the heart of God and extends through the Valley of the Shadow.

But there is also removable suffering, yet such as yields only to years of toil and fatigue and unconquerable faith and perchance only to death itself. The Cross as dogma is painless speculation; the Cross as lived suffering is anguish and glory. Yet God, out of the pattern of His own heart, has planted the Cross along the road of holy obedience. And He enacts in the hearts of those He loves the miracle of willingness to welcome suffering and to know it for what it is—the final seal of His gracious love. I dare not urge you to your Cross. But He, more powerfully, speaks within you and me, to our truest selves, in our truest moments, and disquiets us with the world's needs. By inner persuasions He draws us to a few very definite tasks, *our* tasks, God's burdened heart particularizing His burdens in us. And He gives us the royal blindness of faith, and the seeing eye of the sensitized soul, and the grace of unflinching obedience. Then we see that nothing matters, and that everything matters, and that this my task matters for me and for my fellow men and for Eternity. And if we be utterly humble we may be given strength to be obedient even unto death, yea the death of the Cross.

In my deepest heart I know that some of us have to face our comfortable, self-oriented lives all over again. The times are too tragic, God's sorrow is too great, man's night is too dark, the Cross is too glorious for us to live as we have lived, in anything short of holy obedience. It may or it may not mean change in geography, in profession, in wealth, in earthly security. It does mean this: Some of us will have to enter upon a vow of renunciation and of dedication to the "Eternal Internal" which is as complete and as irrevocable as was the vow of the monk of the Middle Ages. Little groups of such utterly dedicated souls, knowing one another in Divine Fellowship, must take an irrevocable vow to live in this world yet not of this world, Franciscans of the Third Order, and if it be His will, kindle again the embers of faith in the midst of a secular world. Our meetings were meant to be such groups, but now too many of them are dulled and cooled and flooded by the secular. But within our meetings such inner bands of men and women, internally set apart, living by a vow of perpetual obedience to the Inner Voice, in the world yet not of the world, ready to go the second half, obedient as a shadow, sensitive as a shadow, selfless as a shadow—such bands of humble prophets can recreate the Society of Friends and the Christian church and shake the countryside for ten miles around.

## V. SIMPLICITY

The last fruit of holy obedience is the simplicity of the trusting child, the simplicity of the children of God. It is the simplicity which lies beyond complexity. It is the naiveté which is the yonder side of sophistication. It is the beginning of spiritual maturity, which comes after the awkward age of religious busyness for the Kingdom of God—yet how many are caught, and arrested in development, within this adolescent development of the soul's growth! The mark of this simplified life is radiant joy. It lives in the Fellowship of the Transfigured Face. Knowing sorrow to the depths it does not agonize and fret and strain, but in serene, unhurried calm it walks in time with the joy and assurance of Eternity. Knowing fully the complexity of men's problems it cuts through to the Love of God and ever cleaves to Him. Like the mercy of Shakespeare, " 'tis mightiest in the mightiest." But it binds all obedient souls together in the fellowship of humility and simple adoration of Him who is all in all.

I have in mind something deeper than the simplification of our external programs, our absurdly crowded calendars of appointments through which so many pantingly and frantically gasp. These do become simplified in holy obedience, and the poise and peace we have been missing can really be found. But there is a deeper, an internal simplification of the whole of one's personality, stilled, tranquil, in childlike trust listening ever to Eternity's whisper, walking with a smile into the dark.

This amazing simplification comes when we "center down," when life is lived with singleness of eye, from a holy Center where the breath and stillness of Eternity are heavy upon us and we are wholly yielded to Him. Some of you know this holy, recreating Center of eternal peace and joy and live in it day and night. Some of you may see it over the margin and wistfully long to slip into that amazing Center where the soul is at home with God. Be very faithful to that wistful longing. It is the Eternal Goodness calling you to return Home, to feed upon green pastures and walk beside still waters and live in the peace of the Shepherd's presence. It is the life *beyond* fevered strain. We are called beyond strain, to peace and power and joy and love and thorough abandonment of self. We are called to put our hands trustingly in His hand and walk the holy way, in no anxiety assuredly resting in Him.

Douglas Steere wisely says that true religion often appears to be the enemy of the moralist. For religion cuts across the fine distinctions between the several virtues and gathers all virtues into the one supreme quality of *love*. The wholly obedient life is mastered and unified and simplified and gathered up into the love of God and it lives and walks among men in the perpetual flame of that radiant love. For the simplified man loves God with all his heart and mind and soul and strength and abides trustingly in that love. Then indeed do we love our neighbors. And the Fellowship of the Horny Hands is identical with the Fellowship of the Transfigured Face, in this Mary-Martha life.

In this day when the burdens of humanity press so heavily upon us I would begin not first with techniques of service but with the most "Serious Call to a Devout Life," a life of such humble obedience to the Inner Voice as we have scarcely dared to dream. Hasten unto Him who calls you in the silences of your heart. The Hound of Heaven is ever near us, the voice of the Shepherd is calling us home. Too long have we lingered in double-minded obedience and dared not the certainties of His love. For Him do ye seek, all ye pearl merchants. He is "the food of grown men." Hasten unto Him who is the chief actor of the drama of time and Eternity. It is not too late to love Him utterly and obey Him implicitly and be baptized with the power of the apostolic life. Hear the words of Saint Augustine, as he rued his delay of commitment to Him. "Too late loved I Thee, O Thou beauty of ancient days, yet ever new! Too late I loved Thee! And behold, Thou wert within and I abroad, and there I searched for Thee; deformed I, plunging amid those fair forms which Thou hadst made. Thou wert with me but I was not with Thee. Things held me far from Thee which, unless they were in Thee, were not at all. Thou calledst and shoutedst, and burstedst my deafness. Thou flashedst, shonest, and scattered my blindness. Thou breathedst odors, and I drew in breath and pant for Thee. I tasted, and hunger and thirst. Thou touchedst me and I burned for Thy peace. When I shall with my whole soul cleave to Thee, I shall nowhere have sorrow or labor, and my life shall live as wholly full of Thee."

## The Blessed Community

When we are drowned in the overwhelming seas of the love of God, we find ourselves in a new and particular relation to a few of our fellows. The relation is so surprising and so rich that we despair of finding a word glorious enough and weighty enough to name it. The word *Fellowship* is discovered, but the word is pale and thin in comparison with the rich volume and luminous bulk and warmth of the experience which it would designate. For a new kind of life-sharing and of love has arisen of which we had had only dim hints before. Are these the bonds of love which knit together the early Christians, the very warp and woof of the Kingdom of God? In glad amazement and wonder we enter upon a relationship which we had not known the world contained for the sons of men. Why should such bounty be given to unworthy men like ourselves?

By no means is every one of our friends seen in this new and special light. A wholly new alignment of our personal relations appears. Some men and women whom we have never known before, or whom we have noticed only as a dim background for our more special friendships, suddenly loom large, step forward in our attention as men and women whom we now know to the depths. Our earlier conversations with these persons may have been few and brief, but now we know them, as it were, from within. For we discern that their lives are already down within that Center which has found us. And we hunger for their fellowship, with a profound, insistent craving which will not be denied.

Other acquaintances recede in significance; we know now that our relationships with them have always been nearer the surface of life. Many years of happy comradeship and common adventures we may have had together, but now we know that, at bottom, we have never been together in the deep silences of the Center, and that we never can be together, there where the light of Eternity shines still and bright. For until they, too, have become wholly God-enthralled, Light-centered, they can be only good acquaintances with whom we pass the time of day. A yearning over them may set in, because of their dimness of vision, but the eye-to-eye relationship of love which binds together those who live in the Center is reserved for a smaller number. Drastically and re-creatively, Fellowship searches friendships, burning, dissolving, ennobling, transfiguring them in Heaven's glowing fire.

Not only do our daily friendships become re-aligned; our religious friends are also seen anew. Many impressions of worth are confirmed, others are reversed. Some of the most active church leaders, well-known for their executive efficiency, people we have always admired, are shown, in the X-ray light of Eternity, to be agitated, half-committed, wistful, self-placating seekers, to whom the poise and serenity of the Everlasting have never come. The inexhaustible self-giving of others of our religious acquaintances we now understand, for the Eternal Love kindles an ardent and persistent readiness to do all things for, as well as through, Christ who strengthens us. In some we regret a well-intentioned, but feverish over-busyness, not completely grounded in the depths of peace, and we wish they would not blur the beauty of their souls by fast motion. Others, who may not have been effective speakers or weighty financiers or charming conversationalists or members of prominent families are found to be men and women on whom the dews of heaven have fallen indeed, who live continuously in the Center and who, in mature appreciation, understand our leaping heart and unbounded enthusiasm for God. And although they are not commissioned to any earthly office, yet they welcome us authoritatively into the Fellowship of Love.

"See how these Christians love one another" might well have been a spontaneous exclamation in the days of the apostles. The Holy Fellowship, the Blessed Community has always astonished those who stood without it. The sharing of physical goods in the primitive church is only an outcropping of a profoundly deeper sharing of a Life, the base and center of which is obscured, to those who are still oriented about self, rather than about God. To others, tragic to say, the very existence of such a Fellowship within a common Life and Love is unknown and unguessed. In its place, psychological and humanistic views of the essential sociality and gregariousness of man seek to provide a social theory of church membership. From these views spring church programs of mere sociability and social contacts. The precious word *Fellowship* becomes identified with a purely horizontal relation of man to man, not with that horizontal-vertical relationship of man to man *in God*.

But every period of profound re-discovery of God's joyous immediacy is a period of emergence of this amazing group inter-knittedness of God-enthralled men and women who know one another *in Him*. It appeared in vivid form among the early Friends. The early days of the Evangelical movement showed the same bondedness in love. The disclosure of God normally brings the disclosure of the Fellowship. We don't create it deliberately; we find it and we find ourselves increasingly within it as we find ourselves increasingly within Him. It is the holy matrix of "the communion of the saints," the body of Christ which is His church. William C. Braithwaite says in the

Rowntree Series, that it was a tragic day when the Quakers ceased to be a Fellowship and became a Society of Friends. Yet ever within that Society, and ever within the Christian church, has existed the Holy Fellowship, the Blessed Community, an *ekklesiola in ekklesia*, a little church within the church.

Yet still more astonishing is the Holy Fellowship, the Blessed Community, to those who are within it. Yet can one be surprised at being *at home*? In wonder and awe we find ourselves already interknit within unofficial groups of kindred souls. A "chance" conversation comes, and in a few moments we know that we have found and have been found by another member of the Blessed Community. Sometimes we are thus suddenly knit together in the bonds of a love far faster than those of many years' acquaintance. In unbounded eagerness we seek for more such fellowship, and wonder at the apparent lethargy of mere "members."

In the Fellowship cultural and educational and national and racial differences are leveled. Unlettered men are at ease with the truly humble scholar who lives in the Life, and the scholar listens with joy and openness to the precious experiences of God's dealing with the workingman. We find men with chilly theologies but with glowing hearts. We overleap the boundaries of church membership and find Lutherans and Roman Catholics, Jews and Christians, within the

Fellowship. We re-read the poets and the saints, and the Fellowship is enlarged. With urgent hunger we read the Scriptures, with no thought of pious exercise, but in order to find more friends for the soul. We brush past our historical learning in the Scriptures, to seize upon those writers who lived in the Center, in the Life and in the Power. Particularly does devotional literature become illuminated, for the *Imitation of Christ*, and Augustine's *Confessions*, and Brother Lawrence's *Practice of the Presence of God* speak the language of the souls who live at the Center. Time telescopes and vanishes, centuries and creeds are overleaped. The incident of death puts no boundaries to the Blessed Community, wherein men live and love and work and pray in that Life and Power which gave forth the Scriptures. And we wonder and grieve at the overwhelmingly heady preoccupation of religious people with problems, problems, unless they have first come into the Fellowship of the Light.

The final grounds of holy Fellowship are in God. Lives immersed and drowned in God are drowned in love, and know one another in Him, and know one another in love. God is the medium, the matrix, the focus, the solvent. As Meister Eckhart suggests, he who is wholly surrounded by God, enveloped by God, clothed with God, glowing in selfless love toward Him—such a man no one can touch except he touch God also. Such lives have a common meeting-point; they live in a common joyous enslavement. They go back into a single Center where they are at home with Him and with one another. It is as if every soul had a final base, and that final base of every soul is one single Holy Ground, shared in by all. Persons in the Fellowship are related to one another through Him, as all mountains go down into the same earth. They get at one another through Him. He is actively moving in all, co-ordinating those who are pliant to His will and suffusing them all with His glory and His joy.

The relation of each to all, through God, is real, objective, existential. It is an eternal relationship which is shared in by every stick and stone and bird and beast and saint and sinner of the universe. On all the wooing love of God falls urgently, persuadingly. But he who, having will, yields to the loving urgency of that Life which knocks at his heart, is entered and possessed and transformed and transfigured. The scales fall from his eyes when he is given to eat of the tree of knowledge, the fruit of which is indeed for the healing of the nations, and he knows himself and his fellows as comrades in Eden, where God walks with them in the cool of the day. As there is a mysterious many-ing of God, as He pours Himself forth into the universe, so there is a one-ing of those souls who find their way back to Him who is their home. And these are in the Holy Fellowship, the Blessed Community, of whom God is the head.

This community of life and love is far deeper than current views based upon modern logic would suppose. Logic finds, beneath every system of thought, some basic assumptions or postulates from which all other items of belief are derived. It is said that those who share in a system of thought are those who hold basic assumptions in common. But these assumptions are of the intellect, subsequent products, efforts to capture and clarify and make intelligible to ourselves and to others some fragment of that immediacy of experience which is the soul of life itself. Such assumptions we must make, but they are experimental, variant, conditioned by our culture period. But Holy Fellowship reaches behind these intellectual frames to the immediacy of experience in God, and seeks contact in this fountain head of real, dynamic connectedness. Theological quarrels arise out of differences in assumptions. But Holy Fellowship, freely tolerant of these important yet more superficial clarifications, lives in the Center and rejoices in the unity of His love.

And this Fellowship is deeper than democracy, conceived as an ideal of group living. It is a theocracy wherein God rules and guides and directs His listening children. The center of authority is not in man, not in the group, but in the creative God Himself. Nor do all members share equally in spiritual discernment, but upon some falls more clearly the revealing light of His guiding will. "Weighty Friends," with delicate attunement both to heaven and to earth, bulk large in practical decisions. It would be a mistake indeed to suppose that Holy Fellowship is chained fast to one political system, or bound up inextricably with the fortunes of any one temporal structure of society. For the swaying fortunes of democracy and of fascism and of communism are of time, but the Fellowship in God is of all times and is eternal. It is certainly true that some temporal systems are more favorable than are others to the flowering of the Fellowship. But within all groups and nations and creeds it springs up, smiling at differences, for, existing in time, it is rooted in the Eternal One.

No single person can hold *all* dedicated souls within his compass in steadfast Fellowship with equal vividness. There are degrees of Fellowship, from wider, more diffused relations of love to nearer, more intense inter-knittedness. As each of us is at a point in space which compels us to a perspective relationship to all things, some near, some far, so each of us is dear to some and remote from others in the bonds of love.

Within the wider Fellowship emerges the special circle of a few on whom, for each of us, a particular emphasis of nearness has fallen. These are our special gift and task. These we "carry" by inward, wordless prayer. By an interior act and attitude we lift them repeatedly before the throne and hold them there in power. This is work, real labor of the soul. It takes energy but it is done in joy. But the membership of such special groups is different and overlapping. From each individual the bonds of special fellowship radiate near and far. The total effect, in a living Church, would be sufficient intersection of these bonds to form a supporting, carrying network of love for the whole of mankind. Where the Fellowship is lacking the Church invisible is lacking and the Kingdom of God has not yet come. For these bonds of divine love and "carrying" are the stuff of the Kingdom of God. He who is in the Fellowship is in the Kingdom.

Two people, three people, ten people may be in living touch with one another through Him who underlies their separate lives. This is an astounding experience, which I can only describe but cannot explain in the language of science. But in vivid experience of divine Fellowship it is there. We know that these souls are with us, lifting their lives and ours continuously to God and opening themselves, with us, in steady and humble obedience to Him. It is as if the boundaries of our self were enlarged, as if we were within them and as if they were within us. Their strength, given to them by God, becomes our strength, and our joy, given to us by God, becomes their joy. In confidence and love we live together in Him. On the borders of the experience lie amazing events, at which reputable psychologists scoff, and for which I would not try any accounting. But the solid kernel of community of life in God is in the center of the experience, renewing our life and courage and commitment and love. For daily and hourly the cosmic Sacrament is enacted, the Bread and the Wine are divided amongst us by a heavenly Ministrant, and the substance of His body becomes our life and the substance of His blood flows in our veins. Holy is the Fellowship, wondrous is the Ministrant, marvelous is the Grail.

Frequency of personal contact in this Fellowship is not imperative, although desirable. Weeks and months and even years may elapse, yet the reality remains undimmed. Conversations within the Fellowship gravitate toward Him who is dearer than life itself. Yet the degree of self-disclosure which we are given to make to others is variable with time and place and person. And never is it complete. For as it nears completeness, words no longer help, but hinder, and the final pooling of joy and love in Him is accomplished in the silences of the Eternal.

All friendships short of this are incomplete. All personal relations which lie only in time are open-ended and unfinished, to the soul who walks in holy obedience. Can we make *all* our relations to our fellows relations which pass *through Him?* Our relations to the conductor on a trolley? Our relations to the clerk who serves us in a store? How far is the world from such an ideal! How far is Christian practice from such an expectation! Yet we, from our end of the relationship, can send out the Eternal Love in silent, searching hope, and meet each person with a background of eternal expectation and a silent, wordless prayer of love. For until the life of men in time is, in every relation, shot through with Eternity, the Blessed Community is not complete.

# The Eternal Now and Social Concern

There is an experience of the Eternal breaking into time, which transforms all life into a miracle of faith and action. Unspeakable, profound, and full of glory as an inward experience, it is the root of concern for all creation, the true ground of social endeavor. This inward Life and the outward Concern are truly one whole, and, were it possible, ought to be described simultaneously. But linear sequence and succession of words is our inevitable lot and compels us to treat separately what is not separate: first, the Eternal Now and the Temporal Now, and second, the Nature and Ground of Social Concern.

## 1. THE ETERNAL NOW AND THE TEMPORAL NOW

There is a tendency today, in this generation, to suppose that the religious life must prove its worth because it changes the social order. The test of the importance of any supposed dealing with Eternity is the benefits it may possibly bring to affairs in time. Time, and the enrichment of events in time, are supposed to pass a judgment upon the worth of fellowship with the Eternal. We breathe the air of a generation which, as the old phrase goes, "takes time seriously." Men nowadays take time far more seriously than eternity.

German theology of a century ago emphasized a useful distinction between This-sidedness and Othersidedness, or Here and Yonder. The church used to be chiefly concerned with Yonder, it was oriented toward the world beyond, and was little concerned with this world and its sorrows and hungers. Because the sincere workingman, who suffered under economic privations, called out for bread, for whole-wheat-flour bread, the church of that day replied, "You're worldly-minded, you're crass, you're materialistic, you're oriented toward the Here. You ought to seek the heavenly, the eternal, the Yonder." But the workingman wasn't materialistic, he was hungry; and Marxian socialism promised him just the temporal bread he needed, whereas the church had rebuked him for not hungering for the eternal Bread.

All this is now changed. We are in an era of This-sidedness, with a passionate anxiety about economics and political organization. And the church itself has largely gone "this-sided," and large areas of the Society of Friends seem to be predominantly concerned with this world, with time, and with the temporal order. And the test of the worthwhileness of any experience of Eternity has become: "Does it change things in time? If so, let us keep it, if not, let us discard it."

I submit that this is a lamentable reversal of the true order of dependence. Time is no judge of Eternity. It is the Eternal who is the judge and tester of time.

But in saying this I am not proposing that we leave the one-sidedness of the Here and of time-preoccupation for the equal one-sidedness of the Yonder, nor advocate a lofty scorn of this maimed and bleeding world while we bask serenely upon the sunny shores of the Eternal. But I am persuaded that in the Quaker experience of Divine Presence there is a serious retention of both time and the timeless, with the final value and significance located in the Eternal, who is the creative root of time itself. For "I saw also that there was an ocean of darkness and death, but an infinite ocean of light and love which flowed over the ocean of darkness."

The possibility of this experience of Divine Presence, as a repeatedly realized and present fact, and its transforming and transfiguring effect upon all life—this is the central message of Friends. Once discover this glorious secret, this new dimension of life, and we no longer live merely in time but we live also in the Eternal. The world of time is no longer the sole reality of which we are aware. A second Reality hovers, quickens, quivers, stirs, energizes us, breaks in upon us and in love embraces us, together with all things, within Himself. We live our lives at two levels simultaneously, the level of time and the level of the Timeless. They form one sequence, with a fluctuating border between them. Sometimes the glorious Eternal is in the ascendancy, but still we are aware of our daily temporal routine. Sometimes the clouds settle low and we are chiefly in the world of time, yet we are haunted by a smaller sense of Presence, in the margin of consciousness.

But, fluctuating in predominance though the two levels be, such a discovery of an Eternal Life and Love breaking in, nay, always there, but we were too preoccupied to notice it, makes life glorious and new. And one sings inexpressibly sweet songs within oneself, and one *tries* to keep one's inner hilarity and exuberance within bounds lest, like the men of Pentecost, we be mistaken for men filled with new wine. Traditional Quaker decorum and this burning experience of a Living Presence are only with the greatest difficulty held together! I'd rather be jolly Saint Francis hymning his canticle to the sun than a dour old sobersides Quaker whose diet would appear to have been spiritual persimmons.

But now let us examine the ordinary experience of time, unrevised by this great discovery of the Eternal Life springing up within it. The ordinary man, busy earning a living, exercises care, caution, foresight. He calculates probabilities. He studies the past in order to predict and control the future. Then when

he has weighed all his factors and plotted the outcome, with energy and industry he wills himself into
persistent activity along the lines of calculated wisdom.

And much religious work is carried on in just this
same way. With shrewd and canny foresight religious
people study the past, examine all the factors in the
situation which they can foresee, and then decide
what is wisest to undertake, or what is most congru-
ous with the Christian life described in the Gospels.
Then they breathe a prayer to God to reinforce their
wills and keep them strong in executing their resolve.

In this process, time spreads itself out like a ribbon, stretching away from the *now* into the past, and
forward from the *now* into the future, at the far end
of which stands the New Jerusalem. In this ribbon of
time we live, anxiously surveying the past in order to
learn how to manage the most important part of the
ribbon, the future. The *now* is merely an incidental
dividing point, unstable, non-important, except as by
its unstaying migration we move ahead into the richer
meadows and the greener pastures of the future. This,
I fear, is the all-too-familiar world of all too many
religious men and women, when a deeper and a richer
experience is possible.

The experience of Divine Presence changes all this
familiar picture. There come times when the Presence
*steals upon us*, all unexpected not the product of

agonized effort, and we live in a new dimension of life. You who have experienced such plateaus of glory know what I mean. Out from the plain of daily living suddenly loom such plateaus. Before we know it we are walking upon their heights, and all the old familiar landscape becomes new. The experience of Paul is very true: "The former things are passed away; behold, they are become new." One walks in the world yet above the world as well, giddy with the height, with feather tread, with effortlessness and calm security, meeting the daily routine, yet never losing the sense of Presence. Sometimes these periods are acute and brief, too dazzling to report to anyone. Sometimes they are less elevated but more prolonged, with a milder sense of glory and of lift, yet as surely of a piece with the more acute experience. Such experiences are emotionless, in themselves, but suffuse all emotion with a background of peace, utter, utter peace and security.

The sense of Presence! I have spoken of it as stealing on one unawares. It is recorded of John Wilhelm Rowntree that as he left a great physician's office, where he had just been told that his advancing blindness could not be stayed, he stood by some railings for a few moments to collect himself when he "suddenly felt the love of God wrap him about as though a visible presence enfolded him and a joy filled him such as he had never known before." An amazing timeliness of the Invading Love, as the Everlasting stole about him in his sorrow. I cannot report such a timeliness of visitation, but only unpredictable arrivals and fadings-out. But without doubt it is given to many of richer experience to find the comfort of the Eternal is watchfully given at their crises in time.

In the immediate experience of the Presence, the Now is no mere nodal point between the past and the future. It is the seat and region of the Divine Presence itself. No longer is the ribbon spread out with equal vividness before one, for the past matters less and the future matters less, for the Now contains all that is needed for the absolute satisfaction of our deepest cravings. Why want, and yearn, and struggle, when the Now contains all one could ever wish for, and more? The present Now is not something from which we hurriedly escape, toward what is hoped will be a better future. Instead of anxiety lest the future never yield all we have hoped, lest we fail to contribute our full stint before the shadows of the evening fall upon our lives, we only breathe a quiet prayer to the Now and say, "Stay, thou art so sweet." Instead of anxiety lest our past, our past defects, our long-standing deficiencies blight our well-intentioned future efforts, all our past sense of weakness falls away and we stand erect, in this holy Now, joyous, serene, assured, unafraid. Between the relinquished past and the untrodden future stands this holy Now, whose bulk has swelled to cosmic size, for within the Now is the dwelling place of God Himself. In the Now we are at home at last. The fretful winds of time are stilled, the nostalgic longings of this heaven-born earth-traveler come to rest. For the one-dimensional ribbon of time has loosed its hold. It has by no means disappeared. We live within time, within the one-dimensional ribbon. But every time-now is found to be a continuance of an Eternal Now, and in the Eternal Now receives a new evaluation. We have not merely rediscovered time; we have found in this holy immediacy of the Now the root and source of time itself. For it is the Eternal who is the mother of our holy Now, nay, *is* our Now, and time is, as Plato said, merely its moving image.

The sense of Presence is as if two beings were joined in one single configuration, and the center of gravity is not in us but in that Other. As two bodies, closely attached together and whirling in the air, are predominantly determined by the heavier body, so does the sense of Presence carry within it a sense of our lives being in large part guided, dynamically moved from beyond our usual selves. Instead of being the active, hurrying church worker and the anxious, careful planner of shrewd moves toward the good life, we become pliant creatures, less brittle, less obstinately rational. The energizing, dynamic center is not in us but in the Divine Presence in which we share. Religion is not *our* concern; it is God's concern. The sooner we stop thinking *we* are the energetic operators of religion and discover that God is at work, as the Aggressor, the Invader, the Initiator, so much the sooner do we discover that our task is to call men to *be still and know*, listen, hearken in quiet invitation to the subtle promptings of the Divine. Our task is to encourage others first to let go, to cease striving, to give over this fevered effort of the self-sufficient religionist trying to please an external deity. Count on God knocking on the doors of time. God is the Seeker, and not we alone; He is anxious to swell out our time-nows into an Eternal Now by filling them with a sense of Presence. I am persuaded that religious people do not with sufficient seriousness count on God as an active factor in the affairs of the world. "Behold, I stand at the door and knock," but too many well-intentioned people are so preoccupied with the clatter of effort to do something *for* God that they don't hear Him asking that He might do something *through* them. We may admire the heaven-scaling desires of the tower-builders on the Plain of Shinar, but they would have done better to listen and not drown out the call from heaven with the clang of the mason's trowel and the creaking of the scaffolding.

An invariable element in the experience of Now is that of unspeakable and exquisite joy, peace, serene release. A new song is put into our mouths. No old song ever has caught the glory and the gladness of this Now; no former Now can be drawn upon to give perfect voice to this Now. The well-springs of Life are bubbling up anew each moment. When the angel is troubling the waters, it is no time to stand on the bank and recite past wonders. But the main point is not that a *new song* is put into our mouths; the point is that a new song *is put into* our mouths. We sing, yet not we, but the Eternal sings in us. It seems to me, in the experience of plateau living in the Divine Presence, that the Everlasting is the singer, and not we ourselves, that the joy we know in the Presence is not our little private subjective joy, pocketed away from other men, a private gift from a benevolent and gracious God. It is the joy and peace and serenity which is in the Divine Life itself, and we are given to share in that joy which is eternally within all Nows. The song *is put into* our mouths, for the Singer of all songs is singing within us. It is not we that sing; it is the Eternal Song of the Other, who sings in us, who sings unto us, and through us into the world.

For the holy Now is not something which we, by our activity, by our dynamic energy, overtake or come upon. It is a now which itself is dynamic, which lays hold actively upon us, which breaks in actively upon us and re-energizes us from within a new center. We can count upon this as the only secure dynamic, an all-potent factor in world-events. For the Eternal is urgently, actively breaking into time, working through those who are willing *to be laid hold upon*, to surrender *self*-confidence and *self*-centered effort, that is, self-originated effort, and let the Eternal be the dynamic guide in recreating, through us, our time-world.

This is the first fruit of the Spirit—a joy unspeakable and full of glory.

The second is love. It is second not in importance but merely in order of mentioning. For it is true that in the experience of Divine Presence that which flows over the ocean of darkness is an infinite ocean of light and *love*. In the Eternal Now all men become seen in a new way. We enfold them in our love, and we and they are enfolded together within the great Love of God as we know it in Christ. Once walk in the Now and men are changed, in our sight, as we see them from the plateau heights. They aren't just masses of struggling beings, furthering or thwarting our ambitions, or, in far larger numbers, utterly alien to and insulated from us. We become identified with them and suffer when they suffer and rejoice when they rejoice. One might almost say we become cosmic mothers, tenderly caring for all. But that, I believe, is experienced only in the acutest stages of mystic ecstasy, whereas I have been discussing the experience of milder, less lofty plateaus of glory, prolonged days and even weeks of sense of Presence wherein, as Isaac

Penington would say, the springings of the Life are
ever fresh. In such a sense of Presence there is a vast
background of cosmic Love and tender care for all
things (plants included, I find for myself), but in the
foreground arise special objects of love and concern
and tender responsibility. The people we know best,
see oftenest, have most to do with, these are *reloved*
in a new and a deeper way. Would that we could relove the whole world! But a special fragment is
placed before us by the temporal now, which puts a
special responsibility for our present upon us. The
responsibility arising from our location in space is
very different from our responsibility arising out of
our location in time. For we can journey to distant
places and get a different foreground of objects and
events, but we cannot journey out of our time-now
into a new historical location. The invading Love of
the Eternal Now must break in through us into *this*
time-now.

But what is the content and aim of this yearning
Love, which is the Divine Love loving its way into
and through us to others? It is that they too may
make the great discovery, that they also may find God
or, better, be found by Him, that they may know the
Eternal breaking in upon them and making their lives
moving images of the Eternal Life. It is not reserved
merely for the Father-Love in heaven to grieve over
prodigal sons. Wherever any heart has tasted of the
heavenly Love, there is the Father-Love grieving over

prodigals, there is the shepherd heart yearning over sheep not having a shepherd, not knowing where are the green pastures, not even aware that there are green pastures to find, there is one of the sons of God mourning to see his fellows raking together the sticks and the straws while over their heads is held the crown of life. Heaven's eternal Now within us makes us speak blasphemous things, for we seem to assume the prerogatives of God. But this is a part of that astounding boldness of which I mean to speak under the head of peace—our next main fruit of the spirit.

But first I would point out the new fellowship which is born among those who have found the Love which is in the Eternal Now. For those who have been brought back to the *Principle* within them are exquisitely drawn toward all others who have found the same Principle. The fellowship is not founded upon a common subjective experience, like the fellowship of hay-fever sufferers! It is founded upon a common Object, who is known by them all to be the very Life within them. This is the Reality which removes Quakerism from pure individualism and from pure subjectivism, as it is so commonly and so mistakenly interpreted.

The third element in the experience of Presence, after love and joy, is peace. And I make bold to speak of this, even if at this very hour the tragedies of China and of Spain and of German concentration camps are heavy upon us.

The amazing way that anxieties pass away, when enfolded and quickened by the Presence! The old life of one dimension, lived merely in the ribbon of time, was always a *strained* life. Had we calculated the past correctly? What unforeseen happening in the future can arise and overthrow all our efforts? Strain! Strain! Out of such attitudes are built those lives which get written up in the success-stories of the *American Magazine.* And religious people think they must work hard and please God and make a good record and bring in the kingdom! Has the Nietzschean ideal of the superman, with heroic, world-striding power, hypnotized the church into an over-activistic attitude?

And then comes the sense of Presence. The Eternal Now breaks through the time-nows and all is secure. A sense of absolute security and assurance of being linked with an overcoming Power replaces the old anxieties about the Kingdom. It is a security regarding the individual and regarding the group and regarding the race of men. Then we say, "How could we have been so blind?" For surely all things of value are most certainly made secure through Him! Faith, serene, unbroken, *unhurried* world-conquest by the power of Love is a part of peace.

For the experience of Presence is the experience of peace, and the experience of peace is the experience not of inaction but of power, and the experience of power is the experience of a pursuing Love that loves its way untiringly to victory. He who knows the Presence knows peace, and he who knows peace knows power and walks in complete faith that that objective Power and Love which has overtaken him will overcome the world.

And an immediate corollary to this is the weakening of the merely calculated, rationally planned decisions. When we lived in the one-dimensional time-ribbon we had to think life out all by ourselves. The past had to be read cautiously, the future had to be planned with care. Nothing was to be undertaken unless the calculations showed that success was to be expected. No blind living, no marching boldly into the dark, no noble but ungrounded ventures of faith. We must be rational, sensible, intelligent, shrewd. But then comes the reality of the Presence, and the Now-Eternal is found to underlie and generate all time-temporals. And a life of amazing, victorious faith-living sets in. Not with rattle and clatter of hammers, not with strained eyebrows and tense muscles but in peace and power and confidence we work upon such apparently hopeless tasks as the elimination of war from society, and set out toward world-brotherhood and interracial fraternity in a world where all the calculated chances of success are very meagre.

I said that the rational element in the conduct of life is weakened. But the checking and co-ordinating considerations of reason are not eliminated from life guided by the Presence, replaced by the promptings of the moment. Between the atomistic, unintegrated chaos of the time-nows and the coherent, integrated unity of a rational system, wherein time has lost its meaning—between these two factors reflective men have always sought to effect a marriage. Surrender to the promptings of the Eternal Now may involve the absurd courage of faith in the face of insuperable obstacles. But it does not release us from all intelligent and rational and co-ordinated behavior, all reasoning and consistency. Speaking of his openings Fox said he found that "they answered one another and answered the scriptures." There is a unity and coherence and rational continuity in the out-cropping guidances of Spirit-led men. Penn, at the time of the Wilkinson-Story separation, wrote concerning the antinomian claims of the separatists: "As if the Light were inconsistent with itself, or admitted of unity under not only different but contrary practices in the one family and flock of God." This matter needs very careful and much fuller sifting. But I am sure that the outcome must be such that reason and intelligence are not eliminated from those lives who live within the Presence, nor on the other hand are reasoning and intellectual calculations to replace or paralyze the vigor and imperiousness of the Eternal Now.

But in the sense of Presence some of the past nows of our time-now change their character entirely. Our old failures are so apt to paralyze us. The Eternal

Now may counsel: "Undertake this." Our time-now says: "See what a weakling you proved yourself to be in an earlier case. Better not try it now." But the assurance of the Eternal Now is enough, as it should have been for Moses: "Surely I shall be with thee." Submit yourself to the Eternal Now and in peace serene, in the boldness of perfect faith, you can advance into miraculous living. Or, in the opposite direction, our time-now may say: "Do this. You are well prepared for it. Your education and training fit you, perhaps to teach, to preach, to counsel, to guide an enterprise. And if you don't, nobody will." But the Eternal Now in us may say: "Stay. Wait. Don't rely upon yourself. Don't think you can reason yourself into your obligation. Know you not that I can raise up of these stones men better able than you to do this?"

Thus in faith we go forward, with breath-taking boldness, and in faith we stand still, unshaken, with amazing confidence. For the time-nows are rooted in the Eternal Now, which is a steadfast Presence, an infinite ocean of light and love which is flowing over the ocean of darkness and death.

## 2. THE NATURE AND GROUND OF SOCIAL CONCERN

The experience of Divine Presence wholly satisfies, and there are a few who, like those on the Mount of Transfiguration, want to linger there forever and

never return to the valleys of men, where there are
demons to be cast out. But there is more to the experience of God than that of being plucked out of
the world. The fuller experience, I am sure, is of a
Love which sends us out into the world. "As the
Father hath sent me, even so send I you" becomes,
not an external, Biblically authorized command, but
a living, burning experience. For the experience of an
inflooding, all-enfolding Love, which is at the center
of Divine Presence, is of a Love which *embraces all
creation*, not just our little, petty selves. "Would that
all men might be even as I am," are the words of a
man such as John Hughes used to call an *authentic.*
Not only does all creation have a new smell, as Fox
found, but it has a new value, as enwrapped in the
infinite Love of God, wherein not a sparrow falls to
the ground without the Father. Have you *experienced*
this concern for the sparrow's fall? This is not just
Jesus' experience. Nor is it His *inference about God's*
tender love; it is *the record of His experience in God.*
There is a tendering of the soul, toward *everything*
in creation, from the sparrow's fall to the slave under
the lash. The hard-lined face of a money-bitten finan-
cier is as deeply touching to the *tendered* soul as are
the burned-out eyes of miners' children, remote and
unseen victims of his so-called success. There is a
sense in which, in this terrible tenderness, we become
one with God and bear in our quivering souls the sins

and burdens, the benightedness and the tragedy of the creatures of the whole world, and suffer in their suffering, and die in their death.

This is the experience underlying Kagawa's poem, "To Tears," published in the *Christian Century*:

Ah tears! Unbidden tears!
Familiar friends since childhood's lonely years,
Long separated we,
Why do ye come again to dwell with me?

At midnight, dawn, midday
Ye come; nor wait your coming nor delay;
Nay fearless, with what scorn
Ye picture China by my brothers torn.

Your scorn I must accept,
But I'm no coward; pray heed ere more ye've wept;
I love Japan so fair,
And China too; this war I cannot bear.

"Is there no other way?"
Thus do I search my spirit all the day
Nor ever reach a goal;
I live, but only as a phantom soul.

Like Christ who bore our sins upon the Cross,
I, too, must bear my country's sins and dross;
Land of my love! Thy sins are grievous to be borne,
My head hangs low upon my form forlorn.

> Ah tears! Unbidden tears!
> Long separated we,
> Alas! has come another day
> When ye must dwell with me.

This is the voice of an *authentic*, who knows the tendering of the Presence, a tendering which issues in the burden-bearing, cross-carrying, Calvary-re-enacting life.

Against this cosmic suffering and cosmic responsibility we must set the special responsibility experienced in a *concern*. For a Quaker concern particularizes this cosmic tenderness. It brings to a definite and effective focus in some concrete task all that experience of love and responsibility which might evaporate, in its broad generality, into vague yearnings for a golden Paradise.

There are two ways in which a concern is a particularization. It is a particularization of the Divine Concern of God for all creation. God's love isn't just a diffused benevolence. As the Eternal is the root and ground of all times, yet breaks into particular moments, so the Infinite Love is the ground of all creatures, the source of their existence, and also knows a tender concern for each, and guides those who are sensitive to this tender care into a mutually supporting Blessed Fraternity.

But it is a particularization of *my* responsibility

also, in a world too vast and a lifetime too short for me to carry all responsibilities. My cosmic love, or the Divine Lover loving within me, cannot accomplish its full intent, *which is universal saviourhood,* within the limits of three score years and ten. But the Loving Presence does not burden us equally with all things, but considerately puts upon each of us just a few central tasks, as emphatic responsibilities. For each of us these special undertakings are our share in the joyous burdens of love.

Thus the state of having a concern has a foreground and a background. In the foreground is the special task, uniquely illuminated, toward which we feel a special yearning and care. This is the concern as we usually talk about it or present it to the Monthly Meeting. But in the background is a second level, or layer, of universal concern for all the multitude of good things that need doing. Toward them all we feel kindly, but we are dismissed from active service in most of them. And we have an easy mind in the presence of desperately real needs which are not our direct responsibility. We cannot die on *every* cross, nor are we expected to.

Behind the foreground, behind the background, we may distinguish the Ultimate Background, which is the Eternal Concernedness of Love, anterior to its differentiation into the multitude of particulars of creation.

I wish I might emphasize how a life becomes simplified when dominated by faithfulness to a few concerns. Too many of us have too many irons in the fire. We get distracted by the intellectual claim to our interest in a thousand and one good things, and before we know it we are pulled and hauled breathlessly along by an over-burdened program of good committees and good undertakings. I am persuaded that this fevered life of church workers is not wholesome. Undertakings get plastered on from the outside because we can't turn down a friend. Acceptance of service on a weighty committee should really depend upon an answering imperative within us, not merely upon a rational calculation of the factors involved. The concern-oriented life is ordered and organized from within. And we learn to say *No* as well as *Yes* by attending to the guidance of inner responsibility. Quaker simplicity needs to be expressed not merely in dress and architecture and the height of tombstones but also in the structure of a relatively simplified and co-ordinated life-program of social responsibilities. And I am persuaded that *concerns* introduce that simplification, and along with it that intensification which we need in opposition to the hurried, superficial tendencies of our age.

We have tried to discover the grounds of the social responsibility and the social sensitivity of Friends. It is not in mere humanitarianism. It is not in mere pity.

It is not in mere obedience to Bible commands. It is not in anything earthly. The social concern of Friends is grounded in an experience—an experience of the Love of God and of the impulse to saviourhood inherent in the fresh quickenings of that Life. Social concern is the dynamic Life of God at work in the world, made special and emphatic and unique, particularized in each individual or group who is sensitive and tender in the leading-strings of love. A concern is God-initiated, often surprising, always holy, for the Life of God is breaking through into the world. Its execution is in peace and power and astounding faith and joy, for in unhurried serenity the Eternal is at work in the midst of time, triumphantly bringing all things up unto Himself.

## The Simplification of Life

The problem we face today needs very little time for its statement. Our lives in a modern city grow too complex and overcrowded. Even the necessary obligations which we feel we must meet grow overnight, like Jack's beanstalk, and before we know it we are bowed down with burdens, crushed under committees, strained, breathless, and hurried, panting through a never-ending program of appointments. We are too busy to be good wives to our husbands, good homemakers, good companions of our children, good friends to our friends, and with no time at all to be friends to the friendless. But if we withdraw from public engagements and interests, in order to spend quiet hours with the family, the guilty calls of citizenship whisper disquieting claims in our ears. Our children's schools should receive our interest, the civic problems of our community need our attention, the wider issues of the nation and of the world are heavy upon us. Our professional status, our social obligations, our membership in this or that very important organization, put claims upon us. And in frantic fidelity we try to meet at least the necessary minimum of calls upon us. But we're weary and breathless. And we know and regret that our life is

[ 112 ]

slipping away, with our having tasted so little of the peace and joy and serenity we are persuaded it should yield to a soul of wide caliber. The times for the deeps of the silences of the heart seem so few. And in guilty regret we must postpone till next week that deeper life of unshaken composure in the holy Presence, where we sincerely know our true home is, for *this* week is much too full.

But we must not spend precious time merely stating the problem. And although we all enjoy feeling sorry for ourselves, we must not linger long, bewailing the poverty of life induced by the overabundance of our opportunities. Nor must we rush hastily at a solution, breathlessly anxious for once to get something, this day, to show for the time we've spent upon our problem. Prune and trim we must, but not with ruthless haste and ready pruning knife, until we have reflected upon the tree we trim, the environment it lives in, and the sap of life which feeds it.

Let me first suggest that we are giving a false explanation of the complexity of our lives. We blame it upon the complex environment. Our complex living, we say, is due to the complex world we live in, with its radios and autos, which give us more stimulation per square hour than used to be given per square day to our grandmothers. This explanation by the *outward* order leads us to turn wistfully, in some moments, to thoughts of a quiet South Sea Island existence, or to the horse and buggy days of our great grandparents, who went, jingle bells, jingle bells, over the crisp and ringing snow to spend the day with *their* grandparents on the farm. Let me assure you, I have tried the life of the South Seas for a year, the long, lingering leisure of a tropic world. And I found that Americans carry into the tropics their same madcap, feverish life which we know on the mainland. Complexity of our program cannot be blamed upon complexity of our environment, much as we should like to think so. Nor will simplification of life follow simplification of environment. I must confess that I chafed terribly, that year in Hawaii, because in some respects the environment seemed too simple.

We Western peoples are apt to think our great problems are external, environmental. We are not skilled in the inner life, where the real roots of our problem lie. For I would suggest that the true explanation of the complexity of our program is an inner one, not an outer one. The outer distractions of our interests reflect an inner lack of integration of our own lives. We are trying to be several selves at once, without all our selves being organized by a single, mastering Life within us. Each of us tends to be, not a single self, but a whole committee of selves. There is the civic self, the parental self, the financial self, the religious self, the society self, the professional self, the literary self. And each of our selves is in turn a rank individualist, not co-operative but shouting out his vote loudly for himself when the voting time comes. And all too commonly we follow the common American method of getting a quick decision among conflicting claims within us. It is as if we have a chairman of our committee of the many selves within us, who does not integrate the many into one but who merely counts the votes at each decision, and leaves disgruntled minorities. The claims of each self are still pressed. If we accept service on a committee on Negro education, we still regret we can't help with a Sunday-school class. We are not integrated. We are distraught. We feel honestly the pull of many obligations and try to fulfill them all.

And we are unhappy, uneasy, strained, oppressed, and fearful we shall be shallow. For over the margins of life comes a whisper, a faint call, a premonition of richer living which we know we are passing by. Strained by the very mad pace of our daily outer burdens, we are further strained by an inward uneasiness, because we have hints that there is a way of life vastly richer and deeper than all this hurried existence, a life of unhurried serenity and peace and power. If only we could slip over into that Center! If only we could find the Silence which is the source of sound! We have seen and known some people who seem to have found this deep Center of living, where the fretful calls of life are integrated, where No as well as Yes can be said with confidence. We've seen such lives, integrated, unworried by the tangles of close decisions, unhurried, cheery, fresh, positive. These are not people of dallying idleness nor of obviously mooning meditation; they are busy carrying their full load as well as we, but without any chafing of the shoulders with the burden, with quiet joy and springing step. Surrounding the trifles of their daily life is an aura of infinite peace and power and joy. We are so strained and tense, with our burdened lives; they are so poised and at peace.

If the Society of Friends has anything to say, it lies in this region primarily. Life is meant to be lived from a Center, a divine Center. Each one of us can live such a life of amazing power and peace and serenity, of integration and confidence and simplified multiplicity, on one condition—that is, *if we really want to*. There is a divine Abyss within us all, a holy Infinite Center, a Heart, a Life who speaks in us and through us to the world. We have all heard this holy Whisper at times. At times we have followed the Whisper, and amazing equilibrium of life, amazing effectiveness of living set in. But too many of us have heeded the Voice only at times. Only at times have we submitted to His holy guidance. We have not counted this Holy Thing within us to be the most precious thing in the world. We have not surrendered *all else*, to attend to it alone. Let me repeat. Most of us, I fear, have not surrendered all else, in order to attend to the Holy Within.

John Woolman did. He resolved so to order his outward affairs as to be, *at every moment*, attentive to that voice. He simplified life on the basis of its relation to the divine Center. Nothing else really counted so much as attentiveness to that Root of all living which he found within himself. And the Quaker discovery lies in just that: the welling-up whispers of divine guidance and love and presence, more precious than heaven or earth. John Woolman never let the demands of his business grow beyond his *real* needs. When too many customers came, he sent them elsewhere, to more needy merchants and tailors. His outward life became simplified on the basis of an inner integration. He found that we can be heaven-led men and women, and he surrendered himself completely, unreservedly to that blessed leading, keeping warm and close to the Center.

I said his outward life became simplified, and used the passive voice intentionally. He didn't have to struggle, and renounce, and strain to achieve simplicity. He yielded to the Center and his life became simple. It was synoptic. It had singleness of eye. "If thine eye be single thy whole body shall be full of light." His many selves were integrated into a single true self, whose whole aim was humbly walking in the presence and guidance and will of God. There was no shouting down of a disgruntled minority by a majority vote among his selves. It was as if there were in him a presiding chairman who, in the solemn, holy silence of inwardness, took the sense of the meeting. I would suggest that the Quaker method of conducting business meetings is also applicable to the conducting of our individual lives, inwardly. The Holy One stood by, in the inner life of John Woolman, as did Jesus when He stood over against the treasury and watched men and women casting their gifts into the treasury.

And under the silent, watchful eye of the Holy One we all are standing, whether we know it or not. And in that Center, in that holy Abyss where the Eternal dwells at the base of our being, our programs, our gifts to Him, our offerings of duties performed are again and again revised in their values. Many of the things we are doing seem so important to us. We haven't been able to say No to them, because they seemed so important. But if we *center down*, as the old phrase goes, and live in that holy Silence which is dearer than life, and take our life program into the silent places of the heart, with complete openness, ready to do, ready to renounce according to His leading, then many of the things we are doing lose their vitality for us. I should like to testify to this, as a personal experience, graciously given. There is a re-evaluation of much that we do or try to do, which is *done for us*, and we know what to do and what to let alone.

Let me talk very intimately and very earnestly with you about Him who is dearer than life. Do you really want to live your lives, every moment of your lives, in His Presence? Do you long for Him, crave Him? Do you love His Presence? Does every drop of blood in your body love Him? Does every breath you draw breathe a prayer, a praise to Him? Do you sing and dance within yourselves, as you glory in His love? Have you set yourselves to be His, and *only* His, walking every moment in holy obedience? I know I'm talking like an old-time evangelist. But I can't help that, nor dare I restrain myself and get prim and conventional. We have too long been prim and restrained. The fires of the love of God, of our love toward God, and of His love toward us, are very hot. "Thou shalt love the Lord thy God with all thy heart and soul and mind and strength." Do we really do it? Is love steadfastly directed toward God, in our minds, all day long? Do we intersperse our work with gentle prayers and praises to Him? Do we live in the steady peace of God, a peace down at the very depths of our souls, where all strain is gone and God is already victor over the world, already victor over our weaknesses? This life, this abiding, enduring peace that never fails, this serene power and unhurried conquest, inward conquest over ourselves, outward conquest over the world, is meant to be ours. It is a life that is freed from strain and anxiety and hurry, for something of the Cosmic Patience of God becomes ours. Are our lives *unshakable*, because we are clear down on bed rock, rooted and grounded in the love of God? This is the first and the great commandment.

Do you *want* to live in such an amazing divine Presence that life is transformed and transfigured and transmuted into peace and power and glory and miracle? If you do, then you can. But if you say you haven't the time to go down into the recreating silences, I can only say to you, "Then you don't *really* want to, you don't yet love God above all else in the world, with all your heart and soul and mind and strength." For, except for spells of sickness in the family and when the children are small, when terrific pressure comes upon us, we find time for what we *really want* to do.

I should like to be mercilessly drastic in uncovering any sham pretense of being wholly devoted to the inner holy Presence, in singleness of love to God. But I must confess that it doesn't take time, or complicate your program. I find that a life of little whispered words of adoration, of praise, of prayer, of worship can be breathed all through the day. One can have a very busy day, outwardly speaking, and yet be steadily in the holy Presence. We do need a half-hour or an hour of quiet reading and relaxation. But I find that one can carry the recreating silences within oneself, *well-nigh all the time*. With delight I read Brother Lawrence, in his *Practice of the Presence of God*. At the close of the Fourth Conversation it is reported of him, "He was never hasty nor loitering, but did each thing in its season, with an even, uninterrupted composure and tranquillity of spirit. 'The time of business,' he said, 'does not with me differ from the time of prayer, and in the noise and clatter of my kitchen, while several persons are at the same time calling for different things, I possess God in as great tranquillity as if I were upon my knees at the blessed sacrament.' " Our real problem, in failing to center down, is not a lack of time; it is, I fear, in too many of us, lack of joyful, enthusiastic delight in Him, lack of deep, deep-drawing love directed toward Him at every hour of the day and night.

I think it is clear that I am talking about a revolutionary way of living. Religion isn't something to be added to our other duties, and thus make our lives yet more complex. The life with God is the center of life, and all else is remodelled and integrated by it. It gives the singleness of eye. The most important thing is not to be perpetually passing out cups of cold water to a thirsty world. We can get so fearfully busy trying to carry out the second great commandment, "Thou shalt love thy neighbor as thyself," that we are under-developed in our devoted love to God. But we must love God as well as neighbor. These things ye ought to have done and not to have left the other only partially done.

There is a way of life so hid with Christ in God that in the midst of the day's business one is inwardly lifting brief prayers, short ejaculations of praise, subdued whispers of adoration and of tender love to the Beyond that is within. No one need know about it. I only speak to you because it is a sacred trust, not mine but to be given to others. One can live in a well-nigh continuous state of unworded prayer, directed toward God, directed toward people and enterprises we have on our heart. There is no hurry about it all; it is a life unspeakable and full of glory, an inner world of splendor within which we, unworthy, may live. Some of you know it and live in it; others of you may wistfully long for it; it can be yours.

Now out from such a holy Center come the commissions of life. Our fellowship with God issues in world-concern. We cannot keep the love of God to ourselves. It spills over. It quickens us. It makes us see the world's needs anew. We love people and we grieve to see them blind when they might be seeing, asleep with all the world's comforts when they ought to be awake and living sacrificially, accepting the world's goods as their right when they really hold them only in temporary trust. It is because from this holy Center we relove people, relove our neighbors as ourselves, that we are bestirred to be means of their awakening. The deepest need of men is not food and clothing and shelter, important as they are. It is God. We have mistaken the nature of poverty, and thought it was economic poverty. No, it is poverty of soul, deprivation of God's recreating, loving peace. Peer into poverty and see if we are really getting down to the deepest needs, in our economic salvation schemes. These are important. But they lie farther along the road, secondary steps toward world reconstruction. The primary step is a holy life, transformed and radiant in the glory of God.

This love of people is well-nigh as amazing as the love of God. Do we want to help people because we feel sorry for them, or because we genuinely love them? The world needs something deeper than pity; it needs love. (How trite that sounds, how real it is!) But in our love of people are we to be excitedly hurried, sweeping all men and tasks into our loving concern? No, that is God's function. But He, working within us, portions out His vast concern into bundles, and lays on each of us our portion. These become our tasks. Life from the Center is a heaven-directed life.

Much of our acceptance of multitudes of obligations is due to our inability to say No. We calculated that that task had to be done, and we saw no one ready to undertake it. We calculated the need, and then calculated our time, and decided maybe we could squeeze it in somewhere. But the decision was a heady decision, not made within the sanctuary of the soul. When we say Yes or No to calls for service on the basis of heady decisions, we have to give reasons, to ourselves and to others. But when we say Yes or No to calls, on the basis of inner guidance and whispered promptings of encouragement from the Center of our life, or on the basis of a lack of any inward "rising" of that Life to encourage us in the call, we have no reason to give, except one—the will of God as we discern it. Then we have begun to live in guidance. And I find He never guides us into an intolerable scramble of panting feverishness. The Cosmic Patience becomes, in part, our patience, for after all God is at work in the world. It is not we alone who are at work in the world, frantically finishing a work to be offered to God.

Life from the Center is a life of unhurried peace and power. It is simple. It is serene. It is amazing. It is triumphant. It is radiant. It takes no time, but it occupies all our time. And it makes our life programs new and overcoming. We need not get frantic. He is at the helm. And when our little day is done we lie down quietly in peace, for all is well.